A Bipolar Journey

Nick J van der Merwe

For Samantha – the most remarkable woman I

know, who stood by me through all seasons.

Acknowledgements

Since this is my first book, I had no idea what I was getting myself into once I started writing it. I struggled through it and at times those around me struggled with me. It has been a long struggle, as this book took me over three years to write – the information and experience contained in this book isn't something I wrote overnight or in a moment of epiphany.

Most of all thanks and appreciation goes my dear wife Samantha, who had to listen to each word I have written in this book at least once and survived the many nights I tossed and turned (and snored) while thinking up new content for the book and mentally editing my own work.

To Dr M, my wonderful psychiatrist who first set me on the road to recovery.

A big thank you to the folks at SADAG, especially Zane and Cassey, who graciously made the organisation's research statistics and other information available for me to use in this work.

I mention the inputs of people throughout my life and I'd like to thank them all from the first to the last – even the ones you wouldn't expect me to thank. All the people and experiences with people I mention in this book have been stakeholders in my wellbeing at some stage and who have or had an interest in my struggle.

Thank you, Bruce Von Eck, who edited this work for me. Without your inputs, this work would never have seen the light of day. Thanks also to my guinea pig readers. I appreciate your time.

Thank you to Mulalo Mushaisano from Innovative Design who designed the cover of the book for me. We've come a long way together.

To you, the reader. Thank you for picking up this book and your imminent struggle getting through it. I sincerely hope that I will relate something valuable to you in some way, even if it is only something to help you realise that you are not alone in your struggle. Good luck.

With all my love.

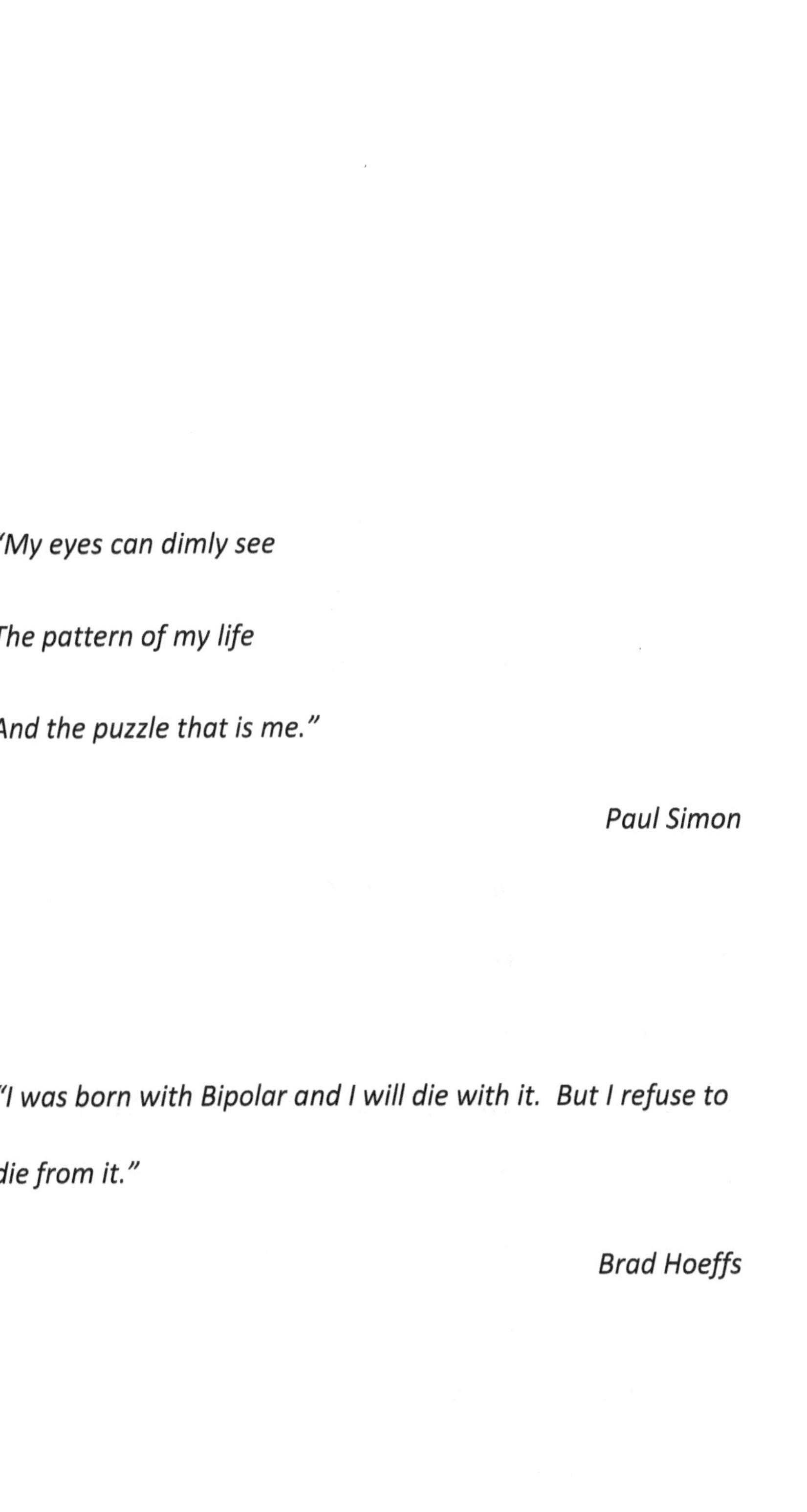

"My eyes can dimly see

The pattern of my life

And the puzzle that is me."

Paul Simon

"I was born with Bipolar and I will die with it. But I refuse to

die from it."

Brad Hoeffs

INDEX

Introduction

You probably wouldn't have picked up this book if you weren't involved with Bipolar in some way or the other – either you or someone you know, may be suffering from the disease. Please keep reading. Bipolar disorder, or Bipolar for short, has been diagnosed in approximately four million South Africans according to research by the South African Depression and Anxiety Group (SADAG). This translates to about one in sixteen people in society being positively diagnosed. The chances of you knowing or interacting with someone with this disease is better than average.

Bipolar is, in short, a physiological illness that presents itself with extreme psychological symptoms: Exaggerated happiness, extreme anger and irritability or anxiety and general emotional instability to name but a few. Then there is the polar opposite of infinite sadness, glumness and, depression only a few can understand.

Bipolar is a very real but highly stigmatised condition – according to research conducted by SADAG, 26% of people are disinterested, lack understanding, and are prejudiced against or even hostile toward people with the disorder. According to the same research, 45% of people with Bipolar have experienced discrimination in the workplace owing to their condition.

These days a lot of people blame some unacceptable behaviour on their supposed *Bipolar disorder.* In fact, it became quite *cool* to have Bipolar over the past few years owing to the number of popular celebrities who claim to have Bipolar. I am reminded of a very famous singer claiming to have Bipolar, who trashed a hotel room and threw a telephone at an employee a couple of years ago. Therefore, some of these stigmas are understandable. These stigmas don't do the person with Bipolar any favours, and more than anything breaks them down into feelings of inferiority and may lead to them experiencing unfair social treatment varying from being ostracised or even being cut off altogether by society or people they know. Even worse is that they may cut themselves off owing to the bad things they've heard about people with Bipolar and a lack of understanding of their condition.

I am aware of many people with Bipolar who live at least quasi-productive lives. We have had proper clinical diagnoses made and had the condition confirmed, in some cases by two, in my case, three different psychiatrists. We face our inner demons head-on and we live with the hand nature dealt us.

Bipolar disorder is a fact like the common cold and there is a plethora of scientific research backing it up. People with Bipolar aren't merely *full of shit* and we can't just *snap out of it*. We don't have the luxury of choosing or knowing how we will feel on any given day. The best we can do is to react and manage those feelings and the triggers in our lives with whatever energy we have.

It may then be my dubious honour to welcome you to the bizarre, sometimes colourful, sometimes shady world of Bipolar. I won't say, "Enjoy your stay", because, like the *Hotel California*, you can never leave. But you can make it a tolerable and interesting world to live in.

I am no authority on Bipolar disorder. Much of what I have written in this book is from my own meandering experience, discussions with other people with Bipolar and reading a lot on the subject. Don't accept everything I say to be an absolute norm or standard; there are just too many angles and aspects in Bipolar to consider, let alone cover them all. Also, please note that I refer to people who *have* Bipolar, not people who *are* Bipolar. Labelling a person *as* Bipolar is, in my opinion, a gross stigmatisation. I have never heard of a cancer patient being called a cancer, so why should it be any different for a person suffering from Bipolar?

The context of this book is mostly oriented to the South African reader, especially when it comes to the legal nitty-gritty. The medicines in Appendix 2 is based on the South African formulary — that is, the medicines which are approved for use in South Africa for the condition at the time of this writing. In other countries, different medicines may or may not be available. It is therefore not a universal standard. Despite these facts, I believe that most of the content in this book regarding the effects of, and living with Bipolar is. Bipolar doesn't discriminate whether you're in South Africa, Japan or Lichtenstein. It also doesn't discriminate between race, class, creed or gender; it takes whoever it can.

Finally, please note that in order to protect myself from prosecution I use the generic names of medicines in this book and not the trade names. To find the trade names you can consult with your psychiatrist or simply Google it.

PART ONE

ME, THROUGH MY OWN EYES

Chapter One

My name is Nick

My name is Nick, how do you do? As I am writing this, I am 40 years old. I have dark brown hair, which is vanishing in some places and greying in some other areas. I am 1.78 metres tall, wear a size 10 boot and my weight oscillates around the 100-kilogram mark. My sense of fashion is slightly out of its time – my wife says it got stuck in the nineties. I wear whatever I'm comfortable in and have little regard for people's opinions as to what I wear. I'll typically wear tidy blue jeans, a golf shirt, and hiking boots. All in all, I won't strike you as unusual, albeit poorly dressed, chubby and balding if you passed me by in the street.

But I also happen to have Bipolar disorder, which is something you won't see if you were judging me by my outward appearances. If I were to meet you in person my introduction would not be, "Hello, my name is Nick and I have Bipolar disorder."

Yet, if I'd let you become a friend you would probably notice that I am not like most people – not that I'm implying that people are the same. Every person is unique; every person has that little something that makes them, *them*. I'm not talking about outward appearances like the colour of their eyes, whether they have freckles or not, whether they prefer KFC to McDonald's, what kind of music they like listening to and superficial stuff like that or the combinations thereof. It often amused me to have read through the singles columns after my divorce after my first marriage where some girl has something she likes and is looking for a decent, handsome guy who is honest, charming, caring and financially secure without attachments, and similar interests. There are probably a gazillion ladies out there with those hopes and needs and a gazillion guys who fit that exact description.

If you were to have me as a friend, you will notice that something is wrong. You will notice that there are times that I won't smile for days on end and just be generally sullen. I wouldn't laugh at your jokes even though I may think they are the funniest thing ever, simply because I don't have the will or energy to laugh. You may find that I isolate myself from you and that the only people I tolerate around me are my very closest family and closest of close friends, who also get snubbed on such days more often than I care to admit.

Other times days will pass where you may think I am the nicest person ever created because I am jovial, always smiling, joking and I seem to have an endless supply of energy. My wife may tell you that I sleep restlessly during these times, talk in my sleep and have extremely vivid dreams. She would know because sometimes I'd wake her up and tell her about them, even though *I'm* fast asleep at the time. I also get fidgety and irritable. I may freak out about the smallest things at home – the empty toilet roll that hasn't been replaced with a new one or is hanging the wrong way around, the toothpaste tube that hasn't been squeezed from the back, an open cupboard door – petty things like that. I may make it very clear to colleagues at work that what they are doing irritates me. Strangely this doesn't happen verbally, but through my body language, which I have difficulty controlling.

There are times I get very forgetful, unreasonable and irrational. There are times that it may seem to you that I am in a state of complete ecstasy or euphoria and there are times you may even think I took recreational drugs.

But what you, even as a friend, won't know, is what happens and where my mind goes when I am all alone by myself. No-one can ever know. Sometimes I don't even know, but I'll try to explain as we go along. All I can tell you is that there is no "happy place," no matter how good or bad it seems to be going.

Anyway, that is enough about me for a moment. I don't want to carry on about myself forever because I don't want to sound like an arrogant megalomaniac. I know I can be one, but this isn't only a memoir; maybe you can buy that in thirty years' time from now if you find this book to be an enjoyable and insightful read. So, it was nice to tell you a bit about myself.

Finally, a big thank you for reading my book. I hope that it helps people with Bipolar, their loved ones and their caregivers as I relate my own story, experiences, and knowledge to you.

Now, let's get down to the nitty-gritty.

Chapter Two

How I came to have Bipolar

The title of this chapter is actually very deceiving. Most people with Bipolar are born with it. Maybe *"The events leading up to my diagnosis"* would be a more appropriate title for this chapter, but I thought it was just a tad too long.

I don't necessarily mean to tell you my life story in this chapter. As I said, I hope I'll have enough experiences to write a worthwhile memoir maybe in thirty years' time. My intention is just to give you an idea of the goings-on in my life, which I think all led up to me eventually being diagnosed with Bipolar. Feel free to skip this chapter; rip it out of the book if you want to, but please recycle the paper.

Many people with Bipolar can trace their first recognisable episode with Bipolar back to a single event that triggered it. I have read and heard about people who finally *cracked* because of stress finally taking its toll: The loss of a loved one or the abuse of drugs or alcohol, two use just two examples. To make a complete list of possible causes will probably take up anything between two and four pages. I really don't want to waste your time by trying to list them, there are just too many of them and they may not even apply to all people who have Bipolar. I probably don't even know a hundredth of the things that can trigger a person's first episode with Bipolar. In my own case I can't distinguish any such single event but understanding myself and my case of Bipolar better now, I can look back on my life and identify a long chain of erratic events linked to it.

Let me try and demystify something about Bipolar right here and right now: Bipolar isn't a psychological condition. It is a physiological condition which presents with psychological symptoms. It is the result of a disorder in the brain, which causes the brain not to produce the correct quantities of chemicals and hormones, mainly serotonin, melatonin, and dopamine, to allow normal transmission of nerve impulses, or communication, between the different areas or synapses of the brain. That basically means that the synapses in the brain are either talking too much or too little at times.

Bear in mind that the brain is an infinitely complex organ. I would venture as far as to say that it is an organ consisting of so many sub-organs that somebody who hasn't studied it extensively can't even begin to understand it. I will venture even further and say that even the most learned medical scientists will be baffled by the intricacies of the human brain for aeons to come.

Thinking back to my childhood and youth, and now that I better understand what was happening to me, I understand so many events so much better. Now that I know that I have Bipolar, looking back I can see the disease running through my life, sometimes like a golden thread and at other times like a length of rusty barbed wire with some of the most beautiful and the most painful memories imaginable.

People with Bipolar do strange, often ludicrous things at the spur of the moment during manic or hypomanic phases, simply because it seems like a good idea at the time. I would often think, "Oh, whatever. This looks like a good idea, I'm going to do this now because it will be fun. I don't care about the consequences and even if there are any, I'm big and strong enough to deal with them. I am unconquerable, all-knowing and invincible!" I also step into the traps of instant gratification with little or no regard or thought of the consequences.

Mom said that from the time I was three days old she just knew that there was something wrong with me. That is apart from what I later heard that she told my grandma in a very emotional telephone call shortly after my birth that I had watery eyes like a fountain-dwelling frog. That old dogma of *mothers knowing* definitely has some merit.

Looking back, the first indication I can recall that I may have had Bipolar happened when I was about four years old. I don't remember all the details and a lot of what I may be writing here is stuff my parents related to me later.

The house we were living in at the time had an inner courtyard between the house and the garage, where the washing line was, and Dad used to park his bike.

It was one afternoon, a Saturday I think, my parents were sitting in the shade having something to drink after some gardening while I was playing around the courtyard. I remember looking at the courtyard wall, about six feet high and decided to charge into it at full speed. I couldn't offer my parents any reason as to why I did it, except that it seemed like a good idea at the time. It left a spectacular mark on my nose though, which could be seen on many of the pictures that were taken of me for months and months afterwards. If you saw pictures of me as a little boy, you would have a hard time believing that such a beautiful boy with those big eyes, wide smile and that sweet angel face was actually harbouring such a terrible disease. I don't know what went wrong with my looks since then.

I have mostly fond memories of growing up. My parents have been married for over 46 years now. I know, more than think, that in the times I grew up in, let alone the world we live in today, that that is no small blessing. Working with kids was my bread and butter: I saw the harsh consequences of single-parent homes every day and it is enough to make a grown man cry; in fact, some days it did.

I am no psychologist, but I think as a child you understand only a few basic emotions or states: Happiness, joy, sadness, guilt, and anger. And of course, to love and not to love and conversely, being loved and not being loved. You may notice that I don't include hate there. I think that most children aren't capable of hate or the comprehension thereof.

I remember experiencing these emotions and states in the superlative degree. When I felt happy, it was beyond elation. When I felt sad, not even my mother could comfort me. And then there were the times that I just flat-lined emotionally. *Beeeeep.*

My school years were less pleasant. I remember experiencing a lot of rejection from my schoolmates in the senior phase of my primary schooling, mainly because I was so *weird* and *different,* which led to rejection, being ostracised and bullied. I believed that popular music was the invention of Satan himself, which didn't exactly endear me to the majority of my peers. People have a natural phobia of anything or anyone who isn't like them. I have always been a rather principled person and I have fought tooth and nail for what I believed in.

I was known as a Bible pusher in junior high school. The two nicknames I had during my time in high school were "Prof" and "Priest". I had a few friends, but not necessarily in a healthy sense of the word. I would latch on to anyone who appeared to have time or sympathy for me. It is in human nature to seek out others like oneself; in my case, I couldn't find anyone at the time, which also exposed me to some less than desirable influences.

I was indeed unusual and strange from other kids' point of view and got so hungry for acceptance that I came to a point of compromising myself and my principles, just wanting to fit in, just craving to be accepted, just desiring to be part the norm, not the exception anymore. I just wanted to be accepted and maybe even loved by my peers. Basically, I wanted to be any Tom, Dick or Harry. But I was Nick, whatever the hell that meant.

Still, winning acceptance was an all-encompassing need for me. I missed out on being a prefect in primary school and I think it may have been the single greatest objective of my high school career – achieving that what was denied me in primary school owing to circumstances beyond my control.

As a teenager, I also became acquainted with new emotions, some more pleasant than others. Feelings like hate, acceptance, and rejection – the most important in my own specific case, and for some reason, I always experienced the rejection stronger than the acceptance. Being the kind of person I am, I soon categorised all feelings, all things into black and white. Life soon became full of dichotomies. Something was either black or white, either right or wrong. Feelings became either positive or negative. I tried convincing myself that black and white are but shades of grey, but I couldn't and to this day I can't.

I came to know many more of these concepts with emotional consequences: Love and hate, joy and sorrow; satisfaction and disappointment; achievement and failure.

I also remember getting distinct episodes of glumness during my high school years. I often felt ill, but not physically. I remember that weeks went by in which I just didn't want to get up, feeling like that apart from becoming a prefect, I had nothing else to achieve. I remember days and weeks passing that I never smiled, and then there were the times I thought I was the funniest person in the grade.

My brother started overtaking me academically and it felt to me that I got out-shined in the only thing I was better at than him. "Damn it all!" I thought. "Why? Why even bother?" He also happened to be very talented on the sports field and until this day I think of him as a very handsome man. He achieved provincial colours in softball and was consistently one of the best players in the league whereas I couldn't even catch a ball until the age of five years old. The only things left for me that I could do better than him was singing in the choir because my brother is almost completely tone-deaf, and play chess, but only slightly better because he did wipe me off the board once or twice. I didn't take those defeats very well.

Speaking of chess, apart from wanting to be a prefect, I learned that I can get school colours for chess if I managed to play in the first team for three years running. It became an obsession to me; I knew I would never get the recognition of provincial colours, but I'd settle for school colours.

At one point I was barely hanging on to my position in the first team and got challenged for my position by the best player in the second team. I lost the play-off, thereby effectively losing my position in the first team and my chances of earning colours. I intensely remember the rage and disappointment I felt at that time and before I could stop myself, I punched the wall so hard that I broke a metacarpal bone in my hand. That wasn't the first or last time I broke or at least injured my hand in an outburst of rage.

1994 was a year of major changes in the lives of all South Africans. It was the year that Apartheid finally went belly up but, in our family, we experienced much more change than a simple change of regime. Dad was retrenched at the end of 1994; he was 44 years old at the time. Put differently, he was an aging white male and at the very lowest step of the affirmative action ladder, his high qualifications in spite. This made his chances of finding new employment quickly very slim.

Mom and Dad decided it may be better to buy a business and spent considerable time travelling the country looking for a promising running concern to purchase. They finally settled on purchasing a fast food restaurant *cum* café in the godforsaken town of Humansdorp in the Eastern Cape Province. It looked like a great running concern at a great price; Dad was able to purchase it from his pension pay-out, which was about R 500,000 at the time.

He took ownership of the business on 1 April 1995, at the end of my first term in Grade 12. My brother had to move down to Humansdorp with Dad and I missed him dearly. My parents insisted I stay in Pretoria to finish my Matric. Apart from it being a bad idea to move a child in a final year from one school to another, I had achieved my goal of becoming a prefect! Mom had to stay behind in Pretoria with me to tie up all the loose ends – selling the house and the likes.

Things finally got wrapped up in June, shortly before the mid-year holidays. I can't remember ever feeling more torn and shattered, bordering on feeling abandoned when she left for Humansdorp too. I understood the reasons for things happening the way it did, but one can't always eliminate the emotion behind it.

Dad managed to scrounge up the money – things were very tight at the time – to come up to Pretoria and he gave me one of two choices: He would either be there for the prize-giving ceremony or for my eighteenth birthday.

I chose to let him come for the prize giving and years later, I realised that rather than wanting acceptance as a person, I wanted recognition and appreciation for my achievements. I won three awards that year: Full colours for chess, full colours for choir singing and the Economic Sciences award for the best combined performance in Accounting and Business Economics. Yet, it felt empty and superficial, like the storming of the Bastille. Storming it, conquering it and finding it practically empty. It felt like all I had done was worked for so long for something that was essentially just an empty shell. I found no fulfilment and no joy in it. My success was an anti-climax and to this day I can't say that I work particularly hard to succeed in what I do – just to spare myself the disappointment. I just work hard now, without any clear result in mind.

I *celebrated* my eighteenth birthday alone – OK, there was my uncle, my aunts, my cousins, my grandma and the two people I considered to be friends. I missed my family so much, especially my brother – would it have been better for me to rather have had Dad there for my birthday? There are just those things in life that shouldn't be the way they are but just can't be helped.

In the end, I graduated from high school with four B symbols, one D symbol and one E. Strangely, I didn't expect a B symbol in Physical Science – I was always trotting along in the D symbol range there. I was appalled by the E symbol for Business Economics; I always had an A symbol for that. So much for the Economic Sciences award. The D for

Mathematics was great because I was merely hoping I'd pass the subject. I was, however, miserable that I missed my distinction in English. Of all the teachers I had in my entire school career, my English teacher was my favourite by far and I felt that I let her down.

I got to go to university – I was one of the 115 students selected for the course I entered for out of almost 1,000 applicants. My parents' finances were extremely tight, but still, they managed to scrape out the money to send me to university and have me live in a hostel. Not one of the university hostels, but a hostel nonetheless.

I remember how I just couldn't get myself to study. There were so many better things to do than attending classes. In fact, the only class I enjoyed was Organisational Psychology, which turned out to be the only subject I passed, by the skin of my teeth, before dropping out of university after just one semester.

I later came to realise that while at university I experienced a major manic episode. I presented with totally irrational behaviour to the point of delusion, which was not entirely a matter of poor self-discipline as I initially thought of it.

Religion became the single most important aspect of my life: I found it more important praying and spending time with Jesus, praising and worshipping at church, finding ways to further the Kingdom of God, so much so that it became a total obsession with me. All I could talk about, think about and bring myself to do anything about was God, Jesus, and more Jesus. Don't get me wrong about disrespecting God and Jesus here; later in this book, there is an entire chapter about God.

To make a long story short, I was so busy with Jesus that He became the all-encompassing obsession of my life. I don't think that that's a bad thing, but there are boundaries – such as when I began to neglect the other things I was supposed to be doing. I was kept at university at a great sacrifice to my parents, and I messed it up. I later learnt that Jesus isn't miraculously going make the knowledge enter my head. Neither was He going to write the exams I blatantly forgot about. Neither would He attend the classes I skipped while I firmly believed I was furthering the Kingdom of God or do any of my assignments while I'm at church evenings because I'm attending evening sessions on counselling and winning souls.

I returned to Humansdorp with my tail tucked between my legs like a whipped dog and a great degree of shame in my heart. I dodged answering questions and giving my report to my parents for a long time. Before I came clean about the semester, Dad would say things like, "You are my pride and joy", and it hurt me so deeply because I knew the disappointment I was going to have to give him before long. If there was a circus or a band in town around that time, I really would have run away with it.

It is said that any business has two sets of books: The one for the actual business operations and another for the taxman to show that the business is making no profit whatsoever. When unscrupulous people are selling a business there must be a third set of books: One showing that the profit margins are off the chart. My parents decided to sell the business after two years for a meagre R 300,000; that was a knock of R 200,000 for two years of blood, sweat, tears and hard labour.

My parents once again went out on a limb for me. Dad had found a job in Pretoria as a lecturer and until this day I'm not sure how they managed to scrape out the money, but we decided that I needed a gap year. I got to go abroad – working on a kibbutz and a moshav in Israel and for the first time in my life, truly experiencing what I thought to be freedom. No Mom or Dad peeking over my shoulder, living the high life. Getting drunk was almost a daily occurrence and the work we were supposed to do was in my opinion merely something to keep us occupied for a while. I grew up on a farm and I knew the meaning of hard physical labour.

I also got introduced to the wonderful, frightening world of illegal drugs and thank goodness I had the good sense, even in my continuing mania, to draw the line at marijuana. But marijuana by itself can be dangerous enough to someone with Bipolar and it should be avoided at all costs, no matter how much fun you remember it to be. Many people will differ with me on this point, but in my own case marijuana drives me into psychosis. I later learnt that there were some rather nasty side effects with marijuana for me once I have started my medication too, like nasty panic attacks.

So, there I was all alone in the great, big, wonderful world. Reclusive on some days and the life of the party some others, but essentially still an outsider. I was still the observer, not a participant and still craving my peers' acceptance. In that kind of environment, there is no recognition for how well you can do what you do and no room for promotion; it is merely about how much fun you can have – how much you can drink, how much marijuana you can smoke and how many women you can bed.

When that was over, could you believe it, when I got back to South Africa, I had another chance to study? I'll leave you to guess what the eventual result of that was.

But I did meet what I believed to be the girl of my dreams. We dated and about two years later we got married. My flawed logic to it, as I later realised, was that when you are done studying and earning a salary, next logical step would be to get married to the person you're with if you are happy together. We had a wonderful wedding ceremony, the kind of which you read in magazines about.

However, married life is no walk in the park – anyone telling you that has probably never been married, is delusional or is trying to sell you a book, a self-help marriage course or counselling.

We soon discovered that money would always be an issue and an obstacle in the way of our hopes and dreams. Around that time, I started to spend money recklessly, hoping to buy my ex's happiness and acceptance. I remember feeling incredibly depressed at times, constantly resorting to buying often nonsensical things to make myself feel better. Later in the book, I talk about mixed states, which is what I must have been experiencing at the time. Mania disguised as depression. I was trying to live the good life while at the same time convincing myself that I was being nice to my ex; a CD here, dinner at an expensive restaurant there, entertaining friends and family while cooking up extremely expensive dinners. They call it retail therapy and so many people walk into that trap: People who can't afford it, like me. The sad part of that is that years later I am still paying those bills, those personal loans, overdrafts and still dodging debt collectors. My ex would always bail me out of trouble, eventually sitting with an overdraft of R 50,000 herself – which was a lot of debt to have at the age of 25 at the time.

Consequently, I started having these grandiose business ideas and I would venture as far as to say that some of them were pretty neat. Yet, I could never find the drive to put my ideas into action because I was paralysed by the fear of failure and until this day I am a pessimist who sees problems in solutions. This gave rise to a cycle of even more grandiose ideas than the previous, which, when the excitement waned, I found a thousand reasons *not* to do that.

A line of that Kenny Rogers song, *"Lucille"* always occurs to me when I recount this specific part of the story, where it says, *"She finally got tired of living on dreams."*

I started working two jobs: Teacher by day, restaurant manager at nights and over weekends. I may have been wrong earlier about me being unable to pinpoint the stage at which I cracked, but it is during this time that I finally realised that something was seriously wrong. "Please get help," my ex pleaded. My parents echoed this cry.

I can't begin to describe how tired I was during that time I worked two jobs. I remember sleeping at school whenever I had a free period, but then working my heart out again over weekends at the restaurant from seven in the morning to ten at night. I also recall getting home at goodness knows what hour and lying in bed, unable to sleep. I remember feeling a lot of resentment from my ex. I felt resented at first for not doing enough to bring in enough money to cover all the debt I had made, and then resented for rarely being at home. Yet I felt incredibly good at the time. I told Dad that for the first time in my life I felt like a dynamic person on my way somewhere. I was juggling so many balls successfully! Or so I thought. I was on my way: I thought it was the road to success, but instead, it turned out to be the highway to hell.

Initially, I thought it was merely a psychological problem, but I happen to be a person who needs to know and understand what is or may be going on with me. I started reading because I have heard of something called "Manic Depressive Illness." *"That might be it,"* I thought. I also read about Borderline Personality Disorder. I learned that the more acceptable term for "Manic Depressive Illness" became "Bipolar disorder". *"Damn,"* I thought. It almost sounds like Multiple Personality Disorder, but that was just a paranoid thought.

Dad recommended that I go see the psychologist he went to see, to see if we could address my problems in some way. Dad blamed and still blames himself for a couple of the whacks of the windmill I have had in my life and asked the psychologist to refer to his records to see if there were any correlations. I don't know whether there were any. I remember walking into the psychologist's office and telling her that I suspected I had either BPD (Bipolar Personality Disorder) or BPD (Borderline Personality Disorder). I thought it to be a hilarious wordplay at the time. Psychologists, except for clinical psychologists, are not qualified to diagnose Bipolar, even though they may suspect it. She referred me to a psychiatrist to have it checked out, but more about that in the next chapter.

Another thing my ex wanted, more than anything in the world, was to be a mother. I was always reluctant about fathering a child because I still wonder after hearing more arguments against my own than I care to remember what favour you do another human soul by bringing them into this world. Not that I didn't want to be a daddy – by no means. After being diagnosed with Bipolar, I was more reluctant to father a child. In my reading, I learnt that the chances of a child having Bipolar are considerably higher when they have a parent who is afflicted.

Nevertheless, we eventually got pregnant and I still think the most beautiful sound I have ever heard was that baby's little heartbeat on the first sonar – 141 beats per minute if I recall it correctly. The pregnancy, however, didn't make it past the first trimester.

Only a man who loves his wife and his unborn child will know what it feels like to hear those dreaded words, "I am afraid I have bad news for you," spoken by the gynaecologist. You know exactly what they mean, but they sound as if they were spoken from a different reality, another universe. Then you see your wife lying on the gynaecologist's bed breaking into a million pieces, weeping uncontrollably and knowing that no words you can ever say or no action on your behalf will ever bring her consolation or comfort.

When I recounted it all later I reached the conclusion that the loss of our unborn baby, I firmly believed it was a girl, was more traumatic to me than our eventual divorce.

It is true that it takes two parties to sink a marriage and I have plenty of theories on some of the reasons why my ex decided to divorce my ass in the end. However, I won't state them here because she will never have the chance to defend herself against my opinions.

The last time I heard anything about her, she had remarried and had the most beautiful baby girl and I am very happy for her that that dream of hers came true. I really wish her years of joy with her daughter and her new husband. I hope he will be better for her than I ever was. I wasn't very nice the last time we had any kind of contact and I don't know how to contact her now and ask her forgiveness or convey these wishes to her. I can only hope she buys or reads this book if she saw my pretty face on the back cover and read these words for herself.

Something I left out which occurred to me after writing the bulk of this chapter is this: Teachers tend to judge themselves by the results of their students. The results I got were less than satisfactory, even alarmingly poor. As a young teacher, I was under permanent scrutiny and had to push myself to get better and better results.

As a result, I had a lot of stress and I was slipping into a deep depression when I got my hands on a packet of Paroxitine. A family member had recently passed away and that was among the stuff we found. I happened to know that Paroxitine is an antidepressant and prescribed it to myself. Stupid me! Little did I know that it would eventually push me over the edge into mania again, and I couldn't care less because at least I was not depressed anymore. Let this be a lesson to one and all: You don't take any CNS (Central Nervous System) acting medicines without consulting a medical practitioner.

Chapter Three

Coming to terms

The first time around that I was writing this specific passage it was very dramatic and as I later came to realise, not entirely the truth. I was neither shocked nor surprised when Dr Doom (my first psychiatrist,) gave me his diagnosis. I refer to him as Dr Doom because he told me what I didn't want to hear.

He had two pairs of glasses which he seemed to interchange from time to time and I could never figure out whether the one pair was for reading and the other for seeing in the midrange. *"Somebody has to tell him about multi-focals at some time or the other,"* I thought. He also had eyes that freaked me out. The one eye's colour didn't match that of the other eye. I just didn't feel comfortable with Dr Doom but that wasn't only about his outward appearances.

"Bipolar," he said. Yet, the word still instilled a holy fear in me as they confirmed my suspicions. As I mentioned, I read up on the condition and I had my suspicions but hearing those words from the mouth of a psychiatrist felt like a death sentence because I knew what it meant. *"Guilty as charged."*

Bipolar. That's the sickness that got people in loony bins, right? How can I afford that? Not the hospitalisation and medication, but I can't afford the loss of income. And how soon will I end up in a hospital and how frequently?

Bipolar. That's the illness that makes you stand in the street and tell any passer-by who cares to listen that Jesus Himself is coming to swim by you just now, right?

OK, the symptoms were there, but no. No, no, no! What did this mean to my job? What did it mean to my marriage or my ability to keep functioning as a member of society?

Or, just, when will the mother ship come and pick me up?

Still, I felt like I had been struck with a sledgehammer right between the eyes: I felt hopeless, helpless and ashamed. Mental disease. So many words milling through my mind: Insane. Lunatic. Maniac. Threat. The list goes on. Ashamed, because I thought something like that could never happen to me. Surely I couldn't have a mental disease or disorder! Yet there, all along, I had it right under my nose, rubbing in my face.

To make the long story short, I was prescribed Carbamazepine CR 400 mg, twice a day, and come see me again two months from now.

A lot of the story and experiences I am trying to relate at this point of time are somewhat sketchy to me. When I was trying to relate it to a good friend of mine, I found that in my own mind the chronology of this part is slightly messed up.

I remember how the Carbamazepine made me flat-line emotionally. *Beeeeep.* Waking up in the morning, no emotional response, not even wanting to maim the alarm clock. Taxis nearly taking me off the road, not even a blink. Driving the mailbox out of the ground without a single emotional reaction. Having my ex telling me she loved me, no reaction as if I had no soul. I felt like I was in a state of mental and emotional zombieness. Something deep inside me screamed, *"This isn't you! You are an emotional being!"*

The grace of it was maybe that I didn't have to deal with having Bipolar. It created a blissful state of denial.

Two months came and went, and it was time to see Dr Doom again. I sat across the desk from him, talking about how the medication made me feel (i.e. nothing at all). He occasionally went "hum," "uhm," and "ah" and finally pushed me a prescription across the desk: Still Carbamazepine CR 400 mg, twice a day, see me in two months. And so started another two months of *"Beeeeep."*

Two months later I saw the man again, and the same happened. *"Well,"* I thought. *"Fuck you and fuck your Carbamazepine."*

Thus began the stage of denial. I just didn't want to be helped. I refused to see another psychiatrist because they were just going to try and zombify me again. I don't want to not have any feelings! I'm a human being, for crying out loud! I need to feel joy! Elation! The wonder of loving and being loved! The grief of mourning, the fulfilment of achieving something no matter how big or small, the disappointment of failure, the things, and emotions that govern the human state, even the appreciation for something as simple as a good cup of coffee.

"Anyway," I told myself: *"I'm not feeling anything anymore, so I'm stable and therefore cured. Crisis averted."* I never went to see Dr Doom again. It was a waste of time anyway and I could have gotten the same prescription from a general practitioner at a better price.

I wanted to write about coming to terms with the illness and here I am rambling on about psychiatrists! Yet, the right psychiatrist is one of the most important aspects in coming to terms with Bipolar, so hear me out. There are only two more psychiatrists to go through and then I'll address what I actually intended this chapter to be about.

I'll tell you about all the other crazy in-between stuff later because it is of a more personal than academic nature – good story reading, but not for kids.

I had not seen a psychiatrist for about a year when disaster struck. This was about the time of my divorce and as can be expected, I was plagued by the deepest, darkest depression. I had no wife to give me her opinion; I only had my parents to rely on for that *outside looking in* perspective. My parents, who had to see their son crumble into a million pieces after his divorce and being unable to pick himself up and putting himself back together again. My parents, who had never given up on me. My parents, who eventually had to endure some of the worst things that a person with Bipolar could throw at you.

Personally, I am very particular when it comes to psychiatrists. I often doubt that the psychiatry they practise is purely clinical in a sense. I have this pathological fear that some psychiatrists are trained to screw around in areas of your mind using less than *kosher* means. I am talking about things on a spiritual level. My parents' pastor recommended me another psychiatrist who, because I knew he had Christian roots, I had more trust in.

Dr J was an old gentleman with kind eyes and who was close to retirement. He was, in my opinion, an infinitely better listener than Dr Doom. He had the proper pathological tests of the thyroid administered and referred me to a psychologist to have an MCMI-III (Millon Clinical Multiaxial Inventory III) analysis done. It is a test consisting of about 180 odd yes or no type questions, the results of which are scarily accurate. Dr J had a look over it and came back with the verdict: Bipolar Type II.

To a greater or lesser extent I felt better, more at peace and comfortable with the diagnosis; maybe because it isn't the first time I heard this diagnosis. I also felt more willing to allow myself to be treated by Dr J.

Normally a patient with Bipolar isn't treated with an anti-depressant only. The typical objective is to stabilise the patient's mood, or brain chemistry then, to a level consistent with what *normal* should be. However, I was heavily depressed at the time. He prescribed an anti-depressant, Moclobemide, only. This worked wonders for some time. I wouldn't say that I snapped out of the depression in no time, but at least I felt able to cope better.

Interestingly, Dr J introduced me to a better mood stabiliser than anything he said he could prescribe – a very effective, simple, over-the-counter supplement: Flaxseed oil. Apart from it being completely natural and harmless to the body, apparently it does a lot to strengthen the integrity of the brain cell membranes, which is useful for the carrying of neuro-impulses. From my own experience and if nothing else, I can tell you that it also does wonders for the immune system – I haven't been down with flu or stomach bugs in ages, apart from the occasional and short-lived cold.

Dr J opted to keep me on Moclobemide for some time and at a later stage when I started exhibiting self-destructive behaviour, he also added Risperidone to my treatment regimen.

What happened next was that there was an incident at my work which put me into severe disrepute and nearly ended up costing me my job. It involved fraud with marks and fingers were pointing at me. The net was tight, yet I knew I was innocent. I recall sitting on some stairs with a pair of compasses and cigarette lighter, heating it and burning MMIX (2009) into my left forearm because I thought of it as the date on my tombstone. I knew that if I couldn't clear my name I would certainly kill myself.

Shortly after I got my name cleared and I thought all was well. Until January of 2010, I think. Here is the part where my crystal ball gets foggy and I can't quite remember what happened.

I recall making an emergency appointment with Dr J to discuss my medication. I clearly remember that the appointment was on a Thursday. I told Dr J that I could feel I was going into mania. However, he thought my own suspicions were ungrounded and left my medication unchanged.

The very next day I slipped into a full-blown mania. It should be understood that there was nothing Dr J could have given me to avert the mania, only to help me cope with it. The episode lasted for anything between four to six months – flowing and ebbing. You can read about it in the next chapter.

When I saw him again, he prescribed Valproic acid and Lamotrigine. I still think of Lamotrigine as a wonder drug for Bipolar, at least in my case. If I recall, I think my initial dosages were 50 mg of Lamotrigine twice a day, and 300 mg Valproic acid evenings. I think that the Lamotrigine eventually got me back onto the rails again. The Valproic acid was later removed from the regimen and we were only left with 50 mg Lamotrigine twice a day. It wasn't a quick fix but in the end, I finally and maybe even for the first time in my life stabilised.

It was good being alive. I wasn't waiting for the mother ship anymore. I wasn't worried about having to keep myself in check all the time. Maybe for the first time in my life, I met *me*.

Dr J retired and I found myself without a psychiatrist again. His patient files were split between two other psychiatrists and my general practitioner recommended the one psychiatrist above the other. Enter my Heaven-sent psychiatrist, Dr M.

I was kept stable on Lamotrigine for quite some time and the first time I consulted her, her judgement was that my condition had gone into remission. Praise be! I could wake up mornings, feel like everyone else feels, go to work and go through my day with the same levels of ups and downs as anyone else. Functionally, I felt like I blended in. I wasn't the guy on the proverbial crutches anymore as I often use the analogy, just the guy with the ankle guard if you could even be bothered to look.

I don't think one can fully appreciate Bipolar without understanding a bit of wave theory, or then, at least some of the terminology: "Frequency," "phase," "amplitude," and "wavelength." Frequency can be expressed as how regularly you cycle. A phase can be an "up phase" (tending toward mania,) or a "down phase" (tending toward depression). Amplitude is how intense the phase is, and wavelength is how long the cycle lasts.

Although Lamotrigine to a great extent sorted out my phases and amplitudes, the frequencies and wavelengths later became erratic. I consulted with Dr M and we increased the dosages to 100 mg twice a day. This caused a huge phase shift, not instantly, but within a week or two, the therapeutic dosage levels were reached in my body. Remember, psychiatric medicine isn't a quick fix and symptoms may often get worse before it gets better. Be that as it may, but about two weeks later I hit an epic depression, which lasted about two weeks.

Yet, I thought all was well after the depression lifted.

The frequencies started mucking around again and we increased the dosages of Lamotrigine to 100 mg mornings and 200 mg evenings. The adaption phase depression followed, slightly worse than the previous, but before I knew it, life was back to normal and it stayed that way for a long time.

Obviously, I thought all was well.

I have no reason for blaming Dr M for what happened next. I am a smoker and have been one since the age of 19, and I think that people with Bipolar are more likely to be addiction-prone than most others. I would like to quit for the sake of my children: I want to spend as much of their lives with them seeing that I missed the first couple of years. I want to grow old enough with my wife that we can smash up our walking canes and use it to start a bonfire on the porch of the old-age home one day. Or live to see my grand-children at the very least.

I knew I was going to need clinical help with that. I've tried going cold turkey before. I've tried hypnosis, and nothing helped. I asked her about Bupropion. I understand that some people have had some level of success with it. I've also learnt the hard way that you don't put any CNS-acting medication in your body without discussing it with your psychiatrist first. Dr M recommended Varenicline instead, and I managed to put down my cigarettes after 13 days, which was quite an achievement even by the standards recommended by the pharmaceutical manufacturer.

The rest of this story you can read about in the next chapter.

The long and short of the story of my psychiatrist is this: For the first time in my life I had a psychiatrist I am completely comfortable with and one whom I feel actually listen to what I'm saying. A psychiatrist isn't a psychologist, but Dr M manages to see the synergy between the two. She isn't just somebody who just sits across the desk from you, listens for a moment to what you have to say (if you're lucky,) and then pulls up a prescription pad and writes you a prescription and say, "Good-bye, take your medication and see me in six months."

She is also the only doctor I ever heard use this phrase: "I am truly sorry for the mistake I made". She hasn't prescribed Varenicline to any patient since then.

I not only respect her for her clinical knowledge and learnedness, but I appreciate her for her humanity, character, can-do attitude and the fact that no matter how crappy I felt, she somehow managed to make me smile. Even on the day I was rearranging her desk before me realising what I was doing.

I understand that all isn't always well, but I now understand why, and I know I've got someone I can trust with my life.

OK, let me (finally) get back to the title of the chapter, *"Coming to terms"*.

Hearing the diagnosis of Bipolar can be extremely disturbing, even if you know what Bipolar is. It can be even more so when you know someone who *has* Bipolar: You've seen what they do, the trouble they can get themselves into and especially, may have endured some of their often-violent mood swings. You've seen how they are sometimes rejected as a nut case and ostracised by society, are glum for days and even end up in the loony bin from time to time.

Then there are those who have never even heard of Bipolar. Hearing a diagnosis you only have little or only sketchy information on is just about one of the scariest things I can think of. It must be a bit like standing on the ledge of a sixty-story building without a guard rail, staring down.

The long and the short of it is this: Once you have been diagnosed, you have two and only two choices: You can decide to go into denial about it or you can accept and even embrace it. I know a bit about what happens when you go into denial, but I can only speculate where that road leads you – you will see where it eventually led me to before pursuing the latter of the two choices. No-one can guarantee that the second road is less bumpy but at least you know where it leads; it enables you to read the road signs and it does a hell of a lot to make life more tolerable for those around you.

If you choose to accept your diagnosis you will have to walk the long and hard path to finding the right combination of medication. It means finding the inner strength of enduring the tempests it causes. It means remaining patient while your brain runs amok with your emotions and subsequently with your relationships with people around you – some you will win, some you will lose.

One of the most important aspects I have found is also to accept that you are not alone. As I pointed out earlier, about four million people in South Africa have Bipolar in one or the other of the plenty of flavours it comes in. Learn to seek them out and befriend such people. Although nobody's case of Bipolar is exactly the same – we have unique personalities for starters – but many other people with Bipolar actually understand what you feel or at least, the mechanisms of it. Sometimes they can even tell you why you feel what you feel. Only another person with Bipolar can really relate to what and how intensely you feel. However, don't get too attached to such a person. They may drag both of you down in the end or conversely, you may drag them down with you.

It is said that one should fight fire with fire. The fire I have found that I can combat my Bipolar with is quite simply knowledge, understanding and medication. I hope that the knowledge I try to dispense in this book proves helpful to you too. Firstly, with the help of your psychiatrist, you need to find out what type of Bipolar you have – there are three main types and an add-on called rapid-cycling. The different types of Bipolar follow different patterns, phases, and intensities. Each patient's patterns are as unique as they are and can therefore not be treated in exactly the same way. No two persons' phases, frequencies, wavelengths or cycles are the same, yet the underlying principles are. Find out what yours are, educate yourself about them and educate those around you; those who form your support structure.

Add to that strength of character. You may know everything there is to know about Bipolar, but if you are not going to apply it in the easiest or most difficult of times, you are doomed to failure.

No person is an island, although with Bipolar it is often OK to ask people sharing the island with you to leave you the hell alone for a bit. This support group is, after your own knowledge and medication, the single most important mechanism for you to deal with your Bipolar. There are clear players with well-defined roles in this support structure; hereafter I will call them your caregivers. In my own case and in no particular order, my caregivers are –

Dr M constantly monitors the physiology of my Bipolar. She is the one who, in the end, makes the decisions about the medications I need to take. It is her job to interpret the rubbish that I am often saying or my body language and prevalent mood states into something meaningful to know what my clinical condition is. It is a job I don't envy her. I sometimes wonder if it isn't also a matter for psychiatrists to ensure they don't give their patients dosages of medication that they can commit suicide with, in extreme cases like my own as you will learn later on.

In some cases, you need a good psychologist. The nature of Bipolar makes it harder and sometimes impossible for us to understand or correctly interpret our emotions and experiences. This often complicates aspects of our lives such as our relationships, and most importantly, our self-esteem and our world view. I started seeing a psychologist because Dr M recommended me to do so. Oh, the boil that was erupting! Why I can't accept anything less than perfect from myself? Why I am always either afraid or angry and therefore irritable? Stuff that I've been hiding away in File

13 of Area 51 for years and years; stuff that I just can't understand, painful stuff. Stuff that I just chose not to think about ever again that had such an enormous impact on my life and on just about everyone I allow close to me.

My parents were the only ones I could count on when my diagnosis was made, and they were the ones who helped me complete the puzzle as it was at that time. Remember, Bipolar is a shapeshifter, always changing its face. I should thank them for kicking my ass hard enough some days to actually do something about my Bipolar. Not all people are as lucky as me to have the parents I do and not everyone with Bipolar has parents who are still alive. In some unfortunate cases, parents just can't or just won't accept the fact that they have a *defective child*. Yet, of all the people in the world, your parents are those most likely to stick with you. Blood is thicker than water, as I have learnt.

A partner, if you have one, is the one person who you should allow to see into the deepest depths of your soul, no matter how messed up it may be. This is the person who requires the greatest degree of honesty from you. Never start a serious relationship with somebody, unless you see yourself playing open cards with them. This includes every aspect from what you feel, why you're feeling that way and especially, that you are suffering from a chronic disease. You need to relate that you suffer from a disease, which requires treatment and can run amok with every aspect of your life from time to time. No matter how much you like a person in the romantic sense of the word if they can't accept these facts they're not worth your time, effort and the devastating heartbreak of both hearts which is bound to follow. Educate your partner about your Bipolar as much as you educate yourself. If you like this book, give it to them to read too. At the end of the day when everyone else is gone, your partner is the one you are left with – eventually to have and to hold, for better or worse, for richer or poorer, *especially* in sickness and health until death do you part.

Dealing with Bipolar often requires superhuman effort and we – and those around us – can't always provide the energy to carry on. That is why I am a firm believer that you should tap into a Higher Power; in my case, I believe in Jesus Christ and I'm not ashamed to say so. Neither am I ashamed to say that anyone who is willing to turn to their Creator, by whichever name you call Him/Her, and ask for help will get it. My purpose with this book is not to sell you on any religion in particular; I am merely telling you what works for me. I have to admit that my relationship with Him is very much influenced by my mood phase. It is sometimes a love/hate relationship, but that is not from His side but mine. All I'm trying to say is that you need your Creator and the power and miracles, not magic tricks, and strength only your Creator can provide to help you. It gets easier with age and maturity and as you get used to the path you walk with Bipolar.

There is one more party left in your circle of caregivers: You. It is impossible to help someone who doesn't want to be helped, including yourself. If you do not want to be helped then you can't help yourself. No-one can. You need to be open and honest with your entire circle of caregivers. In the end, you are the person making the final calls, the base umpire, if you will: Whether you get up or not, whether you exhibit self-restraint or not, self-harm or not, whether you get up and eat, go to work, interact with people and how not. And on some days, whether you live or die. I know this because I've been there more times than I care to admit.

Finally, do yourself the favour and find out who are some of the greatest Bipolar people who ever lived — I'm talking of people like Abraham Lincoln, Isaac Newton, Vincent van Gogh, Virginia Woolf, Charles Dickens, Sylvia Plath, Ludwig von Beethoven, Carrie Fischer, Catherine Zeta-Jones and

Kurt Cobain to name but a few. Don't tell me that these people, for different reasons, made the world we live in today a better place. A bit of Googling sniffs out these names in no time. If you have Bipolar, you find yourself in great company!

Chapter Four

Spiralling out of control

This is so far, the most difficult chapter in the book for me to write. I would have liked to add some humour to this but there isn't any. It is painful to write but the grace of this is that I can remember very little of the content of this chapter. Most of it was related to me by others. I am also writing on some vague recollections, but they feel faint and distant, almost like a light tower in dense fog; the flotsam and jetsam of what remained in my mind. On top of that, there are two *sound clips* from earlier writings which I include to let you form an idea of what goes through my head both during mania and depression. I must also point out that this isn't strictly in chronological order.

I decided to quit my medication about six months into my treatment and I felt half human again after that. I could appreciate my coffee again, get upset and swear at taxis, feel people's love and demonstrate my love for them. I was basically un-zombified but not too long after that, I felt superhuman. I had endless energy, a total disregard for common sense as *normal* people would see it or living in a delusional self-created world where I didn't have a care or rules. Back in the real world, I had plenty of serious things to worry about: My failing marriage, my financial position and my job performance, to name but a few.

My maxed-out credit cards, that I had no idea or care of how to pay off. A total disregard for other people's feelings: They were merely there for my entertainment. To use and abuse people and discard them once you're through with them, in whichever aspect, I'm ashamed to say. And at other times, needing them so much that it hurts, and you hate the world that no-one seems to care about you, not realising that it is because of how I treated them. Or some people, I realised later, that kept me around like a clown because I can be beyond hilarious or delirious at my best.

Driving home so drunk that I couldn't even remember how I got home the next day or driving other people's car at 200 km/h on the highway without their knowledge or consent unless there was a speeding ticket. Or having so many beers that I literally can't stand on my feet anymore and letting a friend without a license drive me home and ending us up in an accident I shouldn't have walked away from. It is nothing short of a miracle that the combination of alcohol and motor vehicles never got me killed.

I don't know if it is a blessing or a curse that I can't remember what happened during manias. All I can say is that when I emerge from mania it is a lot like one of those mornings following a night of heavy drinking and people tell you what you did but without the hangover. When I emerge from a mania I always feel ashamed, not so much about what I did, but the fact that I had little or no control over myself.

While writing this chapter I also read a lot of my earlier writings to give you *sound clips from my mind* such as what I'm like when depressed. It is very difficult to quote something about my manias and I can't do so without summarising many words into few. The quintessential writing during my time was probably this one. Now during manias I often sleep little or nothing; this was written during such a particular night.

*   *   *

(This is edited but notice that I was in a total sensory overload at the time. I'm leaving out most of the music I was listening to while originally writing this, and comments added in italics.)

Sleep is evading me like I evade the city's CBD. Simon & Garfunkel is giving me a private concert on the hi-fi. Since my head is forbidding me to sleep I may as well sit and struggle with whatever it is that I feel is chasing me.

The papers I promised myself will be marked today aren't done. I intended to be in bed by 21:00, but as soon as I put my head down, the papers I was supposed to mark started making an annoying sound like mosquitoes. Subsequently, I got up and finished marking them. In this time, it is after midnight now, I drank two cups of coffee, smoked three cigarettes (I'm strongly considering number four,) calmed the dogs three times and did the dishes.

I'm wrestling with terrible aggression inside of me. It got a hold of me like nasty bronchitis. I lost my self-control with the dogs and their puddles on the ground the previous evening. My *ex* was away for the weekend and when she came back I was sarcastic and abrupt towards her. I don't know what I am so angry about. Is it a frustration that has been lying in rot for too long? Am I holding on to my emotions again? Or is it that I am so sick and tired of all the blows that life has been dealing my *ex* and me the last few years? Come New Years' Eve and we say that it can't be a worse year, but then it is.

01: 37 – Random thoughts

I am sexually frustrated. I quit my restaurant job three weeks ago. I think I may have caught up on lost sleep but now I am beset with an urgency to be busy! Now I am wondering what to do with myself. I must keep busy with something! Anything! This is, of course, a symptom of Bipolar. Maybe that's why I wash dishes at midnight. I will be seeing my psychiatrist *(Dr Doom)* soon. I will ask him to increase my dosages. Everything isn't well. My *ex* says I listen to depressing music. I listened to a lot of music the past weekend since she wasn't here to listen and complain about it.

1:56

Life is precious. So is sleep. My head feels as if it is full of cotton wool. My brain refuses to think. I am tired but I don't want to sleep. I haven't made sense of what is bothering me yet. And I know that as soon as I lay down, it will haunt me again.

The chaos in my life is annoying me. Maybe that's another reason why I washed the dishes around midnight. I am trying to clean up and order and I must keep busy with something, even if it is struggling on paper. I think I have finally achieved an adult level of responsibility. I think my sense of responsibility stopped developing somewhere between the time I was 19 and 21 and in the process, I incurred a lot of damage to myself and others.

The other thing bothering me is this: Some say you know when your time is up. I've heard more than one account of this. The common denominator was that in both cases the person in question was doing a lot of ordering before they died as to minimise the impact of their demise.

2:15

I'll go shower now and then decide if I'll go sleep or if I'll keep writing.

2:30

I need to go diving. Nothing clears my head quite like it, but the problem to the solution is twofold: In the first place, I don't have the money for it and secondly, my *ex* can't get leave anytime soon. Another cup of coffee, then.

2:43 – Random thoughts

Programs on TV irritate me. Somebody, please shoot me! I also resent our dogs. They feel like intruders in my home and then have the gall to pee on the floor, but they also demand time of my *ex*, which I feel I'm not getting enough of. It feels to me that between the fucking TV and the dogs there is no time for me. I had better get active. Since I quit my second job I did reduce my kilojoule intake. I dropped 25 kilograms and I'd like to keep it off.

3:03

Too bad. No more writing and hopefully some sleep.

*   *   *

Notice from this writing that I couldn't follow a logical train of thought. It is just little bits and pieces which occurred at the time of writing this. It is, essentially, a lot of rubbish from a *not fully functional* mind, working in overdrive.

Spiralling out of control could, of course, also mean going to the depressive side of things. I mentioned earlier that my ex and I lost our baby and I only recently realised what a great impact it had on my life. Not too long ago I read something on Facebook which made me break down in tears to such an extent that, being hospitalised for the second time, they had to give me a quite a strong tranquiliser. During the time of one such depression, I wrote this:

*   *   *

Today, in my own biological, physiological and psychological geographical sense, I am Nowhere. I feel so empty today, not only in my head but in my entire being. Like a child, I feel like curling up in a corner somewhere and cry: To cry for the people I knew and aren't there anymore. For the part missing from the world which will make it a better place. I feel like crying about the fact that there isn't water on the moon, about the fact that the Earth is so old and about the fact that I was ever born. Even about the sky that is so blue today.

There is a senseless sorrow emanating from my being that just won't fill the cup of my soul so that it would finally overflow with tears. It remains somewhere between half full and half empty: A mediocrity that only angers me. The Nowhere I am referring to is like the Nothing in *The Never-ending Story* that devours everything, yet contains nothing.

What is inside of me? What is left of me? Was there ever something or am I just like the one incarnation of the Buddha who had to tell himself that he also was merely an illusion? Was I born as a fata morgana? Or was I just a picture or a concept of a person that never existed?

That's where Nowhere is. I am Nowhere. I don't feel anything anymore and the closest I am to any feeling is to feel like crying, but I can't even reach that far.

*   *   *

Notice here that although I was feeling completely and utterly hopeless, depressed and sorrowful, there was some logical train of thought in this writing. It took me the better part of two hours to write because my mind was totally dulled down.

Not too long after that, I had one of the most beautiful experiences in my life and I often refer to it as *the bird that saved my life* when relating the story to others.

Outside the classroom where I was teaching at the time was a beautiful old thorn tree. In that thorn tree, a southern masked weaver was busy building its nest; it was early spring. I watched with fascination how each morning this little bird started building a new nest, as the nest he built the previous day was torn apart by the female. Yet, he would start rebuilding with such joy, such vigour and showmanship that I couldn't help but draw hope from that. I counted five times he rebuilt the nest. Unfortunately, school holidays came, and I don't know what happened to the nest any further. Yet, the joy, resilience, and persistence of that little bird helped, or inspire me at least, to end my depression and gave me a new lease on life at the time. Not that I've never been depressed since, but I will for as long as I live, I will remember that little bird, his joy in the face of adversity.

Back to how messed up I was at the time.

I mentioned earlier how I treated people. I guess I got a little like an unpredictable dog: Kind and gentle the one moment and a deadly machine the next. People who sat out the storm with me through these terrible years hardly speak of it or are kind enough not to. I am in the same way maybe just as relieved as they are that it is over for now. There are no guarantees that it won't ever happen again, but being treated, the chances of relapses like that happening is considerably smaller.

Between the two episodes, I shared about I had a period, I'm not quite sure how long, in which I was relatively stable.

As you know by now, I am a smoker. I want to quit, but I greatly attribute my inability to do so to a great extent to my Bipolar. I tend to get addicted to things quickly and I find quitting them extremely hard. As I mentioned, I asked my psychiatrist to prescribe me Bupropion to aid me in the process. Bupropion is also an anti-depressant and as I pointed out, an anti-depressant isn't normally used in the treatment of Bipolar, unless it is for a very good reason. Instead, she prescribed me Varenicline. She had no way of knowing what the results will be because it was only shortly after my episode with Varenicline that it started having really bad outcomes in clinical trials in terms of even non-psychiatric patients committing suicide.

What happened next my wife calls the Varenicline phase. It was an extremely unpleasant mixed episode because I had an extremely adverse reaction to the Varenicline. At the time the only medication I took for my Bipolar was Lamotrigine, a mood stabiliser for sufferers who tend to have more depressive symptoms. The Varenicline caused me to oscillate between deep depressions and full-blown mania in rapid cycles in ever-increasing frequencies and amplitudes.

Soon, I was incapable of reasonable thought and this came at an extremely inconvenient time, having just married my wife. This led to fierce arguments with my gloves off, saying things I couldn't believe and accusing her directly or indirectly of being a bad mother, among other things – without meaning it, of course. My mouth was just faster than my mind. Soon, a very dark and ugly part of my character I didn't even know existed had taken over my whole being. It felt as if there was another guy in my mind, driving the car. And I didn't like him or the way he drove.

The one night we were in another fierce argument where she was trying to talk some sense into me. I should say that by that time I had already resorted to different forms of self-mutilation: cutting, sticking syringe needles into myself, all for the imaginary reasons of displacing the inner pain and aggression, or as self-punishment – the degree of harm being directly proportional to the graveness of the perceived offense.

I can't remember what was being said but what I do remember is that I started rapping myself against my head with my knuckles and literally screaming, "Do you think that I can't get that into my thick skull!". My wife's expression of shock and horror will haunt me all my days.

I got up and took my car keys with the intention to set off to my parents' house. I knew they weren't there, but I knew where the keys to the safe were kept. I intended to use the opportunity to kill myself. Yet, somehow my wife stopped me.

Something inside me broke that night. I can't remember what day of the week it was, but I remember phoning my Dr M the next day, who made an emergency appointment for me on the Monday morning, after which I was directly hospitalised.

I can't remember ever feeling so lost.

As I am writing this, I am currently under heavy sedation for another mixed episode. I am presently experiencing no emotion whatsoever owing to the medication and it is nothing short of bliss. A mixed manic episode leaves you exhausted both physically and emotionally. This time I was able to detect it in time.

You may also ask what gave rise to my second hospitalisation. Being the open person I am, I will tell you. In my own case, being hospitalised means that things have completely spiralled out of my control.

As you know, I was a teacher. Teachers don't earn the greatest of salaries in South Africa and I was offered a teaching position in Saudi Arabia for about double what I was earning at the time in South Africa. The noble idea behind it was to gather enough money for the kids to be able to go to university, but it didn't turn out that way. There I was, 10,000 kilometres away from home, and not able to get a cent better off than we were – several factors I won't get into now contributing to that, but nonetheless, I wasn't getting ahead financially.

At the time I had to make do with only three to four hours of sleep a night, simply to try to get around to all my duties. That, probably, was trigger number one. Secondly, I got a very bad flu to the extent that I needed four courses of antibiotics to recover, which took the better part of a month. Thirdly, I was working under an enormous amount of stress – I was working mostly with primary school students, who aren't my *forte*. Although I had a fair amount of local social support from other expats, it wasn't my normal tried and tested structure. I couldn't bring myself to open fully nor explain my cycles in detail. Most cycles are learnt by observation anyway.

As a result, I became forgetful, another tell-tale sign that something is up, to the extent that I had to ask a friend to remind me to drink my medication, which he did without fail. I also became overly emotional, one day breaking down in tears in the vice principal's office, him having no idea what Bipolar was and even less what the symptoms were and how it was affecting my work, even if he didn't notice.

My temper started flaring up again and it ended up with me physically dragging a boy out of the class by his leg for throwing a tantrum. In another instance, I screamed at some boys so loudly that apparently I was heard on the other side of the school building. I thought that I was rational at the time and just wanted to give them a good scare, but I now doubt it, knowing now that I was also seeing blood red at the time.

This made me question my reasons for being there in the first place: Working blood, sweat and tears in a rather unpleasant environment, and not having any job satisfaction whatsoever. I began to wonder, even with my reasons for being there, where my place was: Trying to earn my kids a better future than I could have in South Africa, or if it was next to the football field, cheering for my son when he played. On my way home on the airplane I added up the personal cost, and in the end, the balance sheet didn't balance, whichever way I tried to calculate it.

These triggers had pushed me over the edge and there was no stopping it anymore. It was just going from bad to worse. All I eventually had was the support of my wife to see the tell-tale signs of it, albeit from 10,000 kilometres away.

I know my cycles. I knew that when I didn't sleep for at least six to seven hours a night for an extended period, I'll be in for trouble. Normally I can self-medicate that by using my Clobazam during the week to keep myself calm and composed, then making sure I get plenty of sleep over the weekends. I know that if I sleep enough but constantly wake up tired, I'm in for depression. When I sleep dramatically less than six hours a night and wake up feeling rested, I'm in for a mania, especially when I feel rested after that little sleep. When I don't sleep a lot and start needing multiple energy drinks to get me through the day, then there is deep trouble. There is even more trouble when I must start to use the combination of Clobazam and energy drinks to get me through the day.

That's when I got my days and nights switched around and the amount of sleep I got didn't matter anymore because it would always be ineffectual.

Next stop: Hospital.

PART 2

ME, THROUGH CLINICAL EYES

Chapter Five

Diagnosis

I was diagnosed with Type II Bipolar Disorder in 2007 after much prodding from my loved ones to seek out help. Like I said earlier, I didn't want to face the fact that something may be wrong with me, and if there was I was just too arrogant or scared to face it.

I learnt that the main attributes of Type II Bipolar are that it has more hypomanic cycles rather than manic, although mania is possible and that Type II is more prone to depression. I enjoyed the manias at the time of my diagnosis, simply because I felt so good during them. I loved the energy, the creative bursts and the ability to have unbridled fun and laughs. But there were also the lingering depressions, which made the manias and hypomanias seem small and nonsensical in comparison. In my own case, the exchange rate was more or less eight depressive cycles for one mania or hypomania, although in retrospect the manias and hypomanias seemed to last longer than the depressions at the time. Initially, and when I spilled the whole bag of beans to Dr M she said that she may have diagnosed me with Type I Bipolar had I been a patient of her years earlier.

As you saw in the previous chapter, my specific case of Bipolar is something that can have a particularly nasty dragon's head when it wields itself in all its gory glory. People around me got tired of it and although some of them got me to get help, some of them, I think, kept me around for entertainment value until they made me see afterward that people were laughing *at* me, not *with* me.

My case of Bipolar is a particularly nasty kind of shapeshifter to the extent that I need to see my psychiatrist four times per year or in case of emergency, whereas many people see theirs only twice a year. I am fortunate though, because I know of people who must see theirs on a monthly basis or even on a shorter timeframe. In more cases than others, my medication only needs a bit of tweaking, but my check-ups often serve as an early warning system about impending episodes.

I happen to have a rapid cycling case of Bipolar. That means that I sometimes have short periods of time between cycles or that my cycles are shorter more often than not. I can sometimes change from one cycle to the next within a matter of days, sometimes jumping directly from hypomania to a depressive episode or vice versa. Sometimes it even happens in a single day.

When I was a student I had the dream of playing in a band because I found everything else to be empty. I was on quite a mania then and jumped directly into a depression when I realised that that too, would be empty.

There comes my phobia of succeeding once again. I have however found some sort of sense to life and I can gratefully say that I don't believe that I live an empty life anymore.

Again, I've heard another person with Bipolar during one of my hospitalisations say that they experience all four seasons in one day. I count myself fortunate that I don't have it that bad, but there are times I would settle for cycling once a week.

These rapid cycles typically last for a week or two but they are mostly under the dark cloud of depression, with the occasional ray of sunshine breaking through in the form of an extended period of normal days or the occasional hypomanic episode, of which I have little or no recollection afterwards.

Part of my Bipolar surprise package is that I also have a slight case of OCD (Obsessive Compulsive Disorder), a touch of anxiety and Borderline Personality Disorder, but that's something completely different and a whole dynamic by itself which I address later on. My OCD is not so severe that it needs medical treatment, and my anxiety is kept in check by Clobazam when it strikes.

The whole point of this chapter is to illustrate my condition, or at least how well I understand it to the best of my ability. I am finding it difficult to do so, or rather, write a lot about it. Maybe it is because there isn't enough to discuss it in great detail, or I don't quite know how to explain it.

You would have seen up to now and will see some more on how my case of Bipolar presents itself. My diagnosis, to this day, remains a partial mystery to me as if seeing myself through a cracked mirror, neither do I think I will ever fully understand it: Firstly, because I'm not trained to do so, and secondly because there are just too many intricacies to my case, as it is with any other person who has Bipolar.

Anxiety can be a nasty thing, as many people will know. They will often present as so-called panic attacks, but panic attacks can take many forms. It isn't merely limited to shaky hands and sweaty palms. In my case, I pace a lot. Although Bipolar is classified on the schizoaffective side of mental disorders, I am not schizophrenic. And although Bipolar falls into the schizophrenic category of mental disorders, I am not aware of many people, unlike myself, having other schizoaffective disorders too.

I get psychosis from time to time. Psychosis basically happens when you lose touch with reality. It most frequently presents itself with me hearing the dreaded Voices. But then there are also times that I will fear doing the simplest of things like driving. I am often filled with the darkest premonitions of things and what I call an *impending sense of doom* for a specific day.

I can ramble on for hours about my condition or what I perceive it to be without getting down to the clinical facts. This is, however, based on what I know about my condition and the feelings associated with them.

Chapter Six

Treatment

My Bipolar is mainly managed by medication. I take two anti-epileptics, Lamotrigine, and Valproic acid, which together act as a mood stabiliser. I also take an antipsychotic, Risperidone, which is somewhat effective at maintaining my mood or condition at a rather predictable level, although in my case it tends to be slightly on the depressive side of the spectrum; stable, nonetheless. I am prone to bouts of anxiety for which, as needed, I take a mild tranquiliser, Clonazepam. I am also on it chronically when I am being acutely treated for acute mixed manic episodes.

No person with Bipolar can, in my opinion, go at it alone effectively. You need the support structure I spoke about earlier. I think that it is vitally important to have a professional team of a psychologist and psychiatrist in contact with each other. Your trust in them is vitally important. They are, after all dealing with your very life. If you don't feel comfortable with them, you need to change therapists. They are the people who help you manage the psychological and physiological part of the illness.

I have also undergone extensive psychotherapy, but I found that it is to a greater or lesser extent walking around the same bush without getting to the core. Maybe there isn't one in my case, maybe except for what I've discussed in Chapter Two. I found it useful at least to talk to someone who can form a totally objective view of me. I do not wish to disrespect psychotherapists or psychologists in this. I have been and still go to fine psychologists as needed. To name an example, I had a very traumatic experience during the writing of this book, which became a cover story in a newspaper, including a picture of yours truly. I don't know which was worse: The trauma of the event or the intrusion of having my picture on the paper without my consent. To cut a very long story short, my psychologist helped me work through it in a very short time. That's how good she was. She most likely understood that I am most vulnerable on the security level of Maslow's hierarchy. People with Bipolar are from my own experience more prone to *issues* that need dealing with. They aren't merely full of shit and just need more help than most.

My psychiatrist is, as I mentioned, out of this world. She has the ability to actually listen to a person without merely seeing you as just another patient. Not only does she treat a condition, she holistically treats a person.

Equally important is having a support structure of close family or friends or caregivers. Apart from them providing the acceptance and the love we need, they are often also an early warning system for oncoming episodes. I don't hide things from my caregivers – they can only function as an effective part of my life if I am constantly honest about my feelings, informing them on a regular basis what I'm feeling, hurtful or intrusive as they may be. I actually find that by now it has become second nature to do just that. I found that they may even be more important that your healthcare professionals. They see you and interact with you all the time – they are your most important safety net.

As you can see, "treatment" is a broad concept as it ranges from the clinical to the personal. These are intricately intertwined with each other because Bipolar affects you on all levels of your existence. It would seem that the personal care forms the greater part of my treatment owing to the number of people and their efforts involved. I would rather say that it is a 50/50. The clinical treatment, or medications, make it possible for personal care to be effective. You can try to do everything in life, but it wouldn't help when you do the most fundamental of things like breathing. The same goes for medication vs. personal care.

Chapter Seven

Inside the walls

Having Bipolar, or any other mental disease for that matter increases your risk of admission to a psychiatric hospital or institution.

I drove past the clinic in Centurion I was admitted to more times than I care to remember, wondering what lay behind those walls. Were there people walking around in straight jackets, people in rubberised cells or nutcases howling bloodcurdling screams in the middle of the night?

I suppose many of the ideas we harbour about psychiatric hospitals come from the kind of programs we watch on TV – the same kind of stuff that leads us to believe that sharks are cold-hearted, relentless killing machines.

One of the parts for me of coming to terms with Bipolar was that the day may come where I may have to be hospitalised. I only imagined the circumstances under which it happened to be very different. I thought they would literally have to wrestle a gun away from me first or I would enter a catatonic state of depression, or I would be flying so high emotionally to the point of being delusional again.

It didn't quite work the way I imagined it would.

The most stressful parts of being admitted to the hospital when I got hospitalised for the first time were firstly feeling that it was decided on my behalf and secondly, sorting out the medical aid scheme. I'm sure just about anyone reading this will be as familiar as I am that medical aid schemes are happy to receive your money but are full of nonsense when it comes to paying out.

Arriving at the clinic the first time I remember feeling at the same time that I wanted to be there but also planning my escape. I understood that I needed help but not sure if I was able to or rather, willing to, accept that help. I also remember feeling terribly lonely and forsaken – I drove myself to the clinic and no-one was there to see I at least get settled in and comfortable. Not that I blame anyone for it. Life happens. I felt a bit like a condemned man walking the *Green Mile* from the movie by the same title.

When we got to the ward there were an endless series of questions to answer, starting with "How are you feeling today?" *"Like crap, thanks for asking."* Clinical history was determined, blood pressure, weight and an endless series of questions about the things in life causing you stress, what your relationships with your immediate family are like, how strong would you rate this relationship, yadda, yadda, yadda.

"Have you recently attempted or contemplated suicide?"

"Yes. I planned to take a damn gun on Friday night and decorate the ceiling with my brain."

"How frequently do you think about dying?"

"Lately, most of the time."

"Are you feeling suicidal today?"

"For a change not. But that may change in an hour from now."

"On a scale of one to four, which of the following of the list of emotions would you rate as debilitating to you?"

Depression, feelings of worthlessness, hopelessness, anger, paranoia...

Next thing all medication I had with me was confiscated – my Lamotrigine, my Codeine, anti-histamines, muscle rub, antacid: tablets and suspension. Dammit, was I going to try and kill myself with antacid?

Just as a side note: I later learnt that I should avoid painkillers containing Codeine and other opiates altogether. I got a big fright when my Codeine tablets were being counted out and realised that in a matter of 10 days I had gotten addicted to it. The tub of tablets I had with me I had purchased two weeks before I was admitted had 100 tablets in it. Of those tablets, I had 52 or 53 tablets left. I can't recall if I really had any real physical pain during the time, but it still translated to nearly five tablets a day, but I started self-medicating on it and on other more serious pain medications such as Tramadol. I still crave these painkillers to this day and have relapsed into the abuse of Codeine once or twice since that time. Dr M didn't know of my addiction and later advised me not to take any painkillers stronger than Paracetamol or Ibuprofen unless it can be helped.

Night one: I had my new medications as prescribed by Dr M: 100 mg of Lamotrigine, 500 mg of Valproic acid, 10 mg of Clobazam and 10 mg of Zolpidem. At least I slept. On my second trip to a mental hospital, the composition of my medications was still mostly the same except that the dosages were higher than the first time and I had Lorazepam included for the cases of severe agitation and anxiety.

Day two is typically catching up with the routines and schedules: Early appointment with Dr M at 7:40-ish. Breakfast 7:30 – 8:00. Morning *Happy hour:* ASAP after breakfast. Morning sessions 9:00 to 12:00. Lunch 12:30. Afternoon sessions 14:00 to 16:00. Supper 17:30. Psychologists at some random times during the day. Visiting hours from 18:00 to 19:30. Evening rush hour (when you smoke as many cigarettes as you can,) until 20:00, because *lockdown* is from 20:00 to 05:00 the next morning and there was nowhere else you can smoke without getting into severe trouble. Snacks 20:00. Evening *happy hour* 20:30.

Just a note to those who don't know: *Happy hour* is when it is time to drink your medication, which you fetch from the nursing duty station and drink it under the supervision of the nursing staff on duty.

As you can see, a psychiatric clinic can be a busy place at times but also has plenty of idle time too. In the specific clinic where I was there were sessions, which were often insightful, even if it didn't bear a direct reason on why you are hospitalised, but still help you to face your inner demons head-on. There aren't only people in the clinic because they have Bipolar relapses: Contrary to some ideas you as a patient with Bipolar may have, Bipolar isn't the be-all and end-all of mental illnesses. There are people in there for worse things then you are, so count your blessings before you want to feel sorry for yourself. There are people in there for major depression, Post-traumatic Stress Disorder (PTSD), drug and alcohol addiction and Bipolar relapses that may make your troubles seem like minnows.

I still wonder afterwards how much of the healing processes at the clinic I have been to don't happen between the patients, or *"inmates"* as we liked calling each other. Just talking to and just generally caring for each other. There were plenty of smoke breaks and coffee breaks and just talking to the other patients – encouraging each other, discussing points of view, the shape of the universe, what the optimal number of teaspoons of sugar in a cup of coffee is, whether they have ever observed that right-handed people always stir their coffee in a clockwise direction, why we are here, what brought us here, our life stories, another endless list.

I can't tell you how much healing happened at the smoking section, where I spent most of my idle time – years of tears being cried, years of anger and hatred being spat out, people who were cowering like scared puppies getting back onto their feet, people with anger issues calmed down; the list goes on and no, I'm definitely not selling you on the idea of smoking! I am merely sharing my own experiences.

An important aspect of being hospitalised is that you learn that people in the confines and safety of those walls understand what you are going through. You realise that if you were to walk past them in the street you also wouldn't look at them twice just the same way that people would look at you twice. Well, in most of the cases anyway. It is placed into sharp relief to you that are better off but also worse off than some of the inmates and it brings you to the point of counting your blessings; twice in some cases and finding yourself very wealthy indeed.

The saddest part of any day in the clinic was visiting hours – seeing who gets visited and who not. Some of the nicest people I have met in the clinic never had visitors whereas I had visitors almost every day. You sit and you wonder where these folks went, what they thought and what they felt when everyone else's loved ones visited them. It was a topic that was never up for discussion either. The clinic can also be a very lonely place for some.

There is plenty of time for reflection in the clinic and I thought about my children for a great portion of the times I was there. I wrote them each a letter during my first admission, which I hope they'll keep with them to read when things get rough again. In it, I explained a lot of what I feel, how I think, how I feel about them; all the while trying to think how to explain it so they can understand it. It is no small task trying to remember how you thought at a specific age, or even more difficult, how children think who you haven't known all their lives.

Looking back on my experiences in the clinic – I am writing this paragraph while admitted – I can say that they were good timeouts. There is a lot of time to think and to plan your next move in life. The clinic had, in my case, a good way of reminding me what mattered most to me: They are the things you miss first. In my case, my list is, in this order: My wife, then my children, then the rest of my family, and only then my job. And of course, that list also includes a decent cup of coffee in its top ten.

Chapter Eight

Outside the walls

Dad came and picked me up the day I was discharged from the clinic after my first admission. We sat and chatted for almost two hours. Like adults. About the things he thought I needed to change in my life and about the mistakes he saw me making and like any loving father, would like his son not to make. We didn't agree about everything, but I think that that may have been the first truly adult discussion Dad and I ever had.

Driving home, I couldn't believe how little the world had changed in the time I had been hospitalised. The newspaper headlines were still the same: Murder, treason, shame, robbery, theft, and fraud. The same people are still begging at the same traffic lights. Taxis and people who still don't know how to drive on the road.

I will never forget how my daughter was the first there to greet me when I got home – she's normally the last one. I will never forget that beautiful smile and the bright eyes. It was one of the first times really she called me *daddy* – or *Paps*, which was her version of it that one time. When my son saw me, I felt like a tree being scaled by one of these foresters in those silly *Only in America* sports and the absolute joy on his little face.

The unconditional nature of the love of children amazes me – they know, each one of them and in their own way of understanding it, that their daddy has been in the loony bin. Yet, they love me and accept me as I am, grateful for what they have for a daddy, even if he has an obvious crack running straight through the middle.

I don't know if it will always be like that; my daughter won't always be twelve years old like she was at the time of my first discharge and word will get out in her social circles that her daddy is a bit of a cracked nut. And my son will someday realise that his *Superdad's* feet are made of clay, and is an antihero instead of God's blessing to the world the way he may have been thinking about it.

These are the kind of thoughts that scare the hell out of you as a parent with Bipolar. Or even, what if one of my children turns out to have Bipolar? One of my friends recently remarked, "When you get there, cry a river and then build a bridge to cross it."

I keep noticing things about myself which I don't necessarily understand at that moment, and I rely heavily on my wife to relate and to tell me what she sees. She is to a great extent, the one who is leading the blind man by the arm while he is learning to walk with a cane.

Again.

I need her to tell me things like, "It is not a new thing that you have panic attacks. Your reactions to them are just different now." Or, "You may feel like you've lost your sense of balance, mostly because you don't grip things as tightly as you would because you have relaxed a bit." And it wasn't like that after my first hospitalisation either; after my second visit, my grip and sense of balance were also affected. This, of course, had to do with the changes in medication.

In the end, you need to understand that a stay in a hospital isn't a quick fix. There is no quick fix in psychiatric disorders. Institutions and the other private mental clinics are merely service centres where you can get some maintenance done: Have the tyres changed, the gaps in the spark plugs adjusted, and the filters changed. Stuff like that, if you will pardon the metaphor.

Every day outside of the hospital, life becomes easier and the puzzle that is you fall into place, little by little. I needed to find out what worked for me; I am still irritable and agitated and down-right full of social phobia at times. It would still frustrate me endlessly if I went looking for something as simple as a dishcloth on the drying rack and couldn't find one.

But not every day.

My loved ones don't always understand my obsessiveness with the systems I implement to simplify my life and wrestle myself into some kind of routine. You may also find the implementation of routines useful. One of your goals in life should be to make yourself an easier and altogether more congenial person to live with. These changes may, unfortunately, lead to new conflicts you don't need. The hard part for me in those conflict situations is that I just couldn't discern when I am trying to defend my sanity and when I'm just downright being an asshole. I am still utterly confused about that some days.

Ultimately, and by the very nature of Bipolar, I doubt that there is always a balance or a golden midway. It makes me feel like I'm smothering the people, especially my loved ones, around me. Some days you feel like a vine creeper adorning a garden wall; some other days you feel like a dodder plant, latching onto the plants around you like a disease and sapping the life out of them.

In the end, there are only two persons qualified to do the ultimate repairs: Yourself and your Creator, and you need both.

We are here whether you like it or not, whether anyone cares or not. I'm not aware of anyone with Bipolar who asked for it, neither have I heard of any person with diabetes asking for it. What we do with it is up to each one of us individually. That is what each one of our journeys is about: Ultimately the only decision we have to make is how we will approach it.

People with Bipolar are probably some of the greatest liars there are: Suppose that, on average, you get asked how you are four times a day. Most of the time you're *not* fine but you say you are because too few people asking, "How are you?" do it as a mere formality and don't really care. I somehow think that people with Bipolar have a nose for smelling people's sincerity or lack thereof from a mile away. So, as to avoid unwanted conversation or raised eyebrows, you say "Fine, thanks." If we take that "How are you?" is a question you get asked on average four times a day, that then translates to 28 lies per week, 10,220 lies per year and, if we assume you've known that you knew that you had Bipolar since you were eighteen – 429,240 lies by the time you reach 60.

The point is this: You'll never walk out of a mental hospital cured. The hard reality is that you will have to look and see that that hard, cruel world that may have driven you there in the first place is in part still out there – all that may have changed is your perception of it. The world itself hasn't changed one bit and you have to learn to live in it again from scratch. I think it is a bit like learning to walk again. Sometimes it is a day at a time, sometimes it is a step at a time and sometimes it is a breath at a time. The world will always find some shit to throw your way, no matter how bad or how well you are doing. And that goes for all people – the world is good at throwing shit at people.

I think of it as a batsman facing a bowler in cricket – some balls are bouncers, some are on the leg side and most of them on the offside. Some of the balls have an unpredictable spin and some others are just rippers you can't do much about. Just as it is with a batsman, you need a couple of things: Proper protective gear, knowledge of the kinds of balls the bowler may be bowling, knowledge of your own strengths and weaknesses, pads to protect you from the ones you miss, and of course a bat to really whack the ones you can.

Bipolar affects absolutely every area of your life, and by that, I mean everything. It affects the way you feel about yourself on any given day. It affects how you carry or don't carry yourself around people. It affects what you eat, when you eat and how much you eat, even whether you shower or not. It affects your work in the most amazing ways – sometimes very good, sometimes very bad. Most importantly and often in the most devastating ways, Bipolar affects the relationships we have with people.

It has now been a long time since I wrote the bulk of this chapter and I suppose I see many of the things I wrote in this chapter differently now and edited them accordingly. I'm just doing my best to give you a brief overview of what followed on returning to the "real world".

On returning to work (this was after my first admission,) I was three weeks behind the working schedule with five class groups, two groups of them being senior Mathematics, which I had never taught before. It was a very stressful situation and being the kind of person I am, I tend to run like hell and work my fingers to the bone in order to do it right and do it on time. I later explained to someone that I felt like

I'd been dropped onto a running treadmill and never regained my balance all year long.

The senior Mathematics, as it turned out, was no walk in the park and I felt that my head of department was always peeking over my shoulder and always had something negative to say. I tend to be a people pleaser: I like knowing that I do right by other people, especially when it comes to my work. I crave the approval of my superiors because I can't always trust my own opinion of the quality of the work I've done. And when I didn't get it, I became unstable again, feeling worthless, incapable, and a useless waste of space. Dad says that in life you've got to run like hell to stand still in one place and I felt that I was not running fast enough.

It took me five months to catch up, but I was still without the nod of approval I craved from my head of department. With patience and effort, you get a lot of things done. Some of them you will win, some others you will lose.

I had by no means stabilised by the time I was discharged from the hospital on any of my discharges. My medication would still be adapted several times before I am where I am after my first discharge. It isn't an easy road, but if there is something I learnt about myself and other people with Bipolar it is that we are brave. We put on a pair of shoes every day that most people can't begin to fathom what it is like to walk in. When we have decided to walk in them, we do just that and I will keep walking as long as I humanly can.

Chapter Nine

The long, winding road

The title of this book doesn't include the word, "journey", for no reason. It isn't an exaggeration because that is exactly what life with Bipolar is: It is a journey, a voyage, an epic odyssey. You don't know where it may take you or where you will end up, but you can exercise some level of control over it.

With Bipolar you are either relapsing or recovering or in remission, if you are lucky, but you may experience episodes on the road to recovery. I have talked about relapses but let's also talk about recovery. Recovery is a serious matter in Bipolar and in the end, that's where you want to be at: Recovery and ultimately remission. There are no jumps and leaps in it, only baby steps. Recovery doesn't happen overnight, especially if you are in the middle of an episode or even a relapse.

To say it isn't an easy road wouldn't be an understatement. You are bound to be on it for a considerable percentage of the time, if not most of the time until you have been stabilised to a good degree. Recovery doesn't mean stable *per se*. On any road, there are manageable bumps and hills and slopes. There are easy stretches and there are uncomfortable gravelly parts where you will get dirt in your shoes, but it is a road nonetheless. It is not the wilderness of relapse or as I have experienced, going untreated. The roads and the episodes you encounter here can be negotiated considerably easier. You just need to know where you are going and how to read the signs along the road.

Life with Bipolar is a journey, the road that was set before me and everyone with Bipolar, that we have to travel. We have a choice in the matter of how we decide whichever way to travel it, but travel it we must.

It is easy to want to quit on the road to recovery. More often than not, you need to grind your teeth and trudge on, even more so if you are just so tired. But you have to keep moving because it is when you stop moving forward that you start putting yourself in danger of relapses. You should constantly nurture the strength in yourself to keep on moving; some days you will need to tap into that strength and if it isn't there, my friend, you will slide off the road.

Your body is bound to change as you grow older and subsequently, so will its chemistry. Life will keep throwing balls at you, which you may or may not be able to play back. If the road is too slippery you, just like me, will relapse.

I have suffered and will suffer many relapses in my life, maybe even serious enough to end up in the loony bin again – I'm in for my third stint as I am writing this.

It is probable that I will have many more havoc-wreaking changes in my medication. I started out on quite small dosages of medications and I am now at four times the strength of some medications I initially was. You never can be certain because Bipolar is rife with impossible variables.

You don't always know what is around the next bend and you can't always be prepared for it. It is so for every single person with Bipolar and each one would tell you exactly the same thing if you asked them.

In my case, there will always be a depression lurking somewhere in the shadows, I just don't know how severe it may be. There may also be the occasional hypomania or mixed episode. Goodness knows what the consequences thereof may be and how much damage control there may be to do afterwards. Obviously, I am more afraid of those than I am about depression.

For people with Bipolar, every day remains a challenge. There is no way of knowing how you will feel when you wake up, except when you're in a distinct episode for as long as it lasts. At least you are brave enough to play the hand that nature dealt you, to get up and to the best of your abilities play to your strengths. On any given day that may mean a step at a time or even a breath at a time or merely going through the motions on some other days. Whichever way you play it, it takes a courageous effort and immense strength of character which few possess in the world we live in. I daresay that if everybody had the resolve of some people with Bipolar, the world would be a much better place to live in.

There is no quick fix in Bipolar. Know your triggers. Know your strengths and your weaknesses. Play to your strengths and beware your weaknesses as far as you can. Accept that you won't always be able to. Accept that Bipolar is the hand that was dealt to you – the sooner you do that, the sooner you will find yourself on the road to recovery and once there, keep walking with all your strength.

PART THREE

THE EMOTIONAL ROLLER COASTER

Chapter Ten

Depression

A whole chapter on depression? I pity you for having to read this because in this chapter I will be trying to spell out what depression is, more specifically, what it feels like and how dark it can get. Yet, it is virtually impossible to put it into words.

Along the line in life, about one in four people are likely to experience some sort of a depressive episode – usually because of something that can be pinpointed to something such as a traumatic event or great personal loss. Unlike major depression, depression cycles in Bipolar don't always have a clear trigger – they just happen without any clear environmental reason, or it is a part of the biological roller-coaster as I explained it to someone recently.

A while back I read a cartoon stating that Bipolar is waking up and not knowing whether *Eeyore* or *Tigger* from *Winnie the Pooh* will be making your decisions on any particular day.

On the depressive days, it is Eeyore.

Everything, even breathing feels like an effort. Putting one foot in front of the other feels as if it takes a superhuman effort, sapping the energy out of you which you just do not have. Sometimes, making it up out of bed and onto the sofa seems to be a good day's work, to be rewarded with some series and movies on the rare occasion that I really felt up to it. As for me, on such days I crave silence. The pillows go over my head and even the sounds of my breathing and my own heartbeat are unwelcome intruders. On days like these I'm not even talking about the effort it takes to pull the corners of my lips upwards and smile. Forget about it.

Colours are dull and gloomy as if they belong to the musty shadow world of an old museum. Humour, even though I may understand it, becomes intolerable. I get irritated with laughing people – how dare they be happy? Frankly, depressed days are as Douglas Adams put it, *the long, dark teatime of the soul*. There just isn't any tea, though.

Food loses its taste and I don't get hungry for days on end and literally have to force myself to eat something. I don't even feel like cleaning myself up. I stay tired, no matter how much I sleep, and sleep is pretty much the only thing I feel like doing, because when I sleep, I feel that I don't have to fight – I don't have to face the demons; I can just drift off to a generally blissful, dreamless nowhere.

I can't begin to describe how badly, on some days, I just want to roll over and die, or worse, kill myself. The scary part in my case is that on any given day of being depressed, I can find a million ways to kill myself – whether it is hanging myself, slitting my wrists, taking an overdose of my medications or jumping in front of a speeding truck; there will always be a way if you want to die badly enough. Fortunately, one of the times when it was touch and go for me, my wife managed to stop me. Still, where there is a will, there are a million ways.

It is hearing the dreaded Voices telling me what a bad person, what a waste of space and oxygen I am when things are getting really bad.

It is also mostly during depressive spells that I have resorted to self-harm. You just feel so dead inside and cutting yourself, or sticking needles into myself, or burning myself with hot objects is just a way to affirm to myself that I'm still alive. If I hurt or bleed, I must be alive. Self-harm is also a mechanism people may use to project inner pain outwards or self-punishment as I mentioned earlier.

Why am I telling you this? Because it must be one of the freakiest things to know someone is willingly causing themselves pain or harm. I just think that people need to understand what it is about. It's rarely about seeking attention. Volumes have been written on self-harm and I daresay that it is not fully understood yet.

Physiologically my brain doesn't feel functional. In fact — physiologically my brain *isn't* fully functional. It feels like it has the shape, size, and consistency of a walnut. I'm are forgetful and can't follow a train of thought at its normal pace. I have a hard time following a conversation and often have to ask people to repeat what they said. Professionally and socially I try to keep up appearances by going through the motions as best as my brain will allow you to. I keep on saying I'm fine because I think that nobody really gives a damn about how I am feeling, or you can't see that they do at any rate. Speaking for myself, I normally doubt people's ability to care anyway — even more so when I'm depressed.

People say my eyes become dull and cloudy, lifeless as if I'm looking at them from a different reality. This is partially true, except for the reality part. That kind of reality is called hell. Hell like that hurts and the emptiness you are experiencing doesn't exist on this earth, except for that which I'm are carrying inside of me.

It is a very frail emotional state of mind. It is hurtful and I can't seem to understand why I hurt or find a reason why I should hurt. I just do. It feels like razor blades cutting into my heart and my vocal cords and eyeballs. I am constantly fighting to keep back the tears, swallowing the groans and subduing the apparently nonsensical sorrow I feel. It is the sweaty palms and pacing because of the irrational fear and trepidation gripping me that I feel like something terrible is about to happen. It is the decision of taking the next breath, taking the next step and staying alive for another minute. It is being mauled by the Black Dog. I call depression the Black Dog – It is big and ugly and mean.

When I feel the onset of depression I often say that the Black Dog is chasing me. That is the thing about my own depressive cycles – I feel them coming most of the time. Those who know me really well, like my wife, will tell me there is a depression coming on even before I see the Black Dog, simply because they've learnt to read the signs better than I have.

The thing I do like about a depressive episode over a manic or hypomanic episode is that there is a certain sobriety to it.

I can run from it as long as my stubby little legs will allow me, but in the end, it almost always catches up with me. My thoughts, though clouded and annoyingly slow, sometimes make some sort of sense. I can, most of the time, make sense of what I am thinking, even if it is at a half or quarter of the speed I would when I'm in, say, remission or a state of apathy.

Depressive episodes may follow a pattern such as shown in the diagram below; it isn't the be-all and end-all of how depressive episodes look; the long and short of it is that the level of depression may fluctuate over time. You may feel more down the one moment to the next, the one day to the next or one week to the next. There is no set time frame the diagram is purely illustrative.

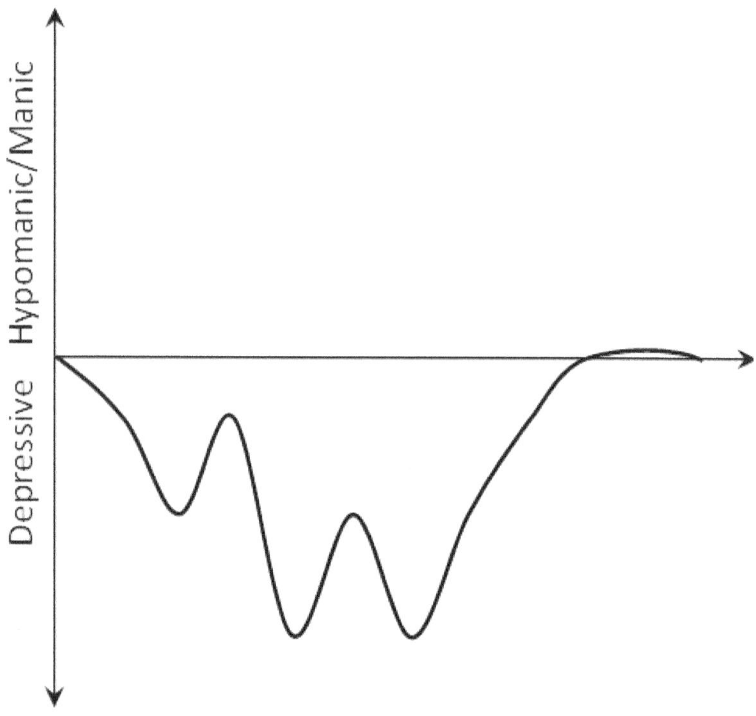

Normally, when depression hits me, it hits hard. Many people don't know this, but depression is the predominant state for both Types I and II Bipolar. That is why uninformed people often perceive us to act out of character when a manic or hypomanic phase strike – it is completely and indeed the exact opposite of what we normally appear to be, where our mood states appear around neutral or toward the depressive side of the spectrum.

Depression is the cycle you are likely to experience the most but it isn't a death sentence. You can still get things done in proportion to the degree of how depressed you are. The important thing is that you keep moving and try not to lie down. Yes, there are times that you'll get so depressed that you don't even feel like getting out of bed – or even can't for that matter – but it is possible to stay productive. That should be your aim.

Finally, lean on your support structure. They are there to prop you up during these times of depression. Remember though that you only need to lean as hard as you should. Propping up a dead weight is very difficult. Remember that those in your support structure are also human; they may get tired and wobble a little. Therefore, provide as much conscious effort as you can to keep your depressions in check as best as you can. It seems to be virtually impossible at times, but if you dig deep enough you will find a great degree of strength. Remember, you are strong. If you weren't, you wouldn't be here to read this.

Chapter Eleven

Mania and hypomania

This chapter should read easier than the previous because it deals with, dare I say, an altogether more pleasant aspect of Bipolar. Or so it will seem. Mania and hypomania make a welcome change from the dull, grey, hopeless existence of depressive episodes. Mania and hypomania are a bright, neon-coloured wonderland with the sparks of fireworks all around.

The first thing people like about a manic or hypomanic episode is the pure and unbridled euphoria of the state. Life rarely gets that good. You have a seemingly endless flow of energy and creative ideas.

In mania and hypomania, colours are beautifully bright, and things taste better. You feel great and can hardly believe that you ever experienced depression. You don't feel the need for a lot of sleep and will often wake up refreshed after just a couple of hours of sleep a day.

In this state, it is Tigger making the decisions. Instead of fleeing from Black Dogs, it is riding on unicorns. It is full of ceaseless energy and cravings for Winnie the Pooh's *hunny*.

Mania and hypomania are often reckless states, or at least, they are in my own case. I say and do things I dearly regret later, simply because my brain is red-lining it and my mouth and actions are following suit. It was remarked to me that during my mania of 2010, I was totally incoherent in my speech, not finishing sentences before starting with the next. During this particular episode or relapse, once again following an afternoon of binge drinking, I thought it will be a particularly good idea to go and practice sliding-in to non-existent softball bases in the gravel parking area of the bar.

Why?

It seemed like a good idea at the time and I was so convincing that I conned some equally drunk friends into doing the same with me. Obviously, I do suffer from psychosis and hallucinations when I am in full-blown mania.

In my case, it is a state where I crave instant gratification. Such as doing softball slides, no matter how painful or reckless it may be, not only to me but to others as well. Whatever seems like a good idea at the time, I'll do if it holds a thrill. I'll often start something that I later have no idea how to finish. It often meant binge drinking in my case; I am aware that other people with Bipolar also take to more serious drugs during such manic or hypomanic episodes.

Some others may engage in irresponsible sexual liaisons, simply because of the thrill of it.

Some people with Bipolar become totally and utterly delusional during these states, experiencing visual and audial hallucinations. That means seeing things that aren't there and hearing the dreaded Voices. I often get the audial hallucinations, but not to the extent that the Voices are telling me what to do, but they sometimes put ideas into my head, which I can recall having but once the episode is over, can't recall the content. Mostly, I would hear my name being called while there is nobody there, which is frightening enough as compared to what other people may say the Voices tell them. Other times it would just sound like walking in a shopping mall and just picking up bits and pieces of conversations as people walk past you, but they are very, very real, especially when I'm alone.

All in all, mania and hypomania are a strange and illogical state to the beholder. Some people with Bipolar enjoy the manic state and will often induce it by not taking their medications, especially when they have been depressed for a while.

On the other hand, I am reading about more and more people disliking mania or hypomania for the simple reason of what they do or are capable of doing in those states. Like I mentioned earlier, mania and hypomania aren't always a pleasant state. I, for one, feel ashamed and guilty merely by recognising that it is coming on, or that I have been in such a state. It is a grace to me that I seldom remember what I said or did while in that state. I am not alone in that regard – other people with Bipolar have also reported it.

The scariest version of mania, as per my own experience is the mixed-manic state. That is when full-blown mania and depression may occur at the same time or in rapidly recurring succession. That is what ended me up in the hospital the first time and looking back, there were several such episodes during the course of my life that have passed untreated and caused major damage. Obviously, I recovered from those without medication, but had I been medicated I would have caused a lot less damage and the relapse would have been shorter or manageable at least.

If I were to illustrate a manic or hypomanic phase, it may look like the following diagram; the same criteria applying as with the illustration on depression earlier.

The dashed line applies to Type II Bipolar and the solid line to Type I. Note that Type II can experience full-blown mania too, just not as frequently and probably not as intense.

Something else worth pointing out is that people with Bipolar can experience *depression* during mania or hypomania. This may happen when their mood level dips below their usual emotional level in the state – this has happened to me, ending up with me looking for help for depression while I was actually in a long hypomanic phase.

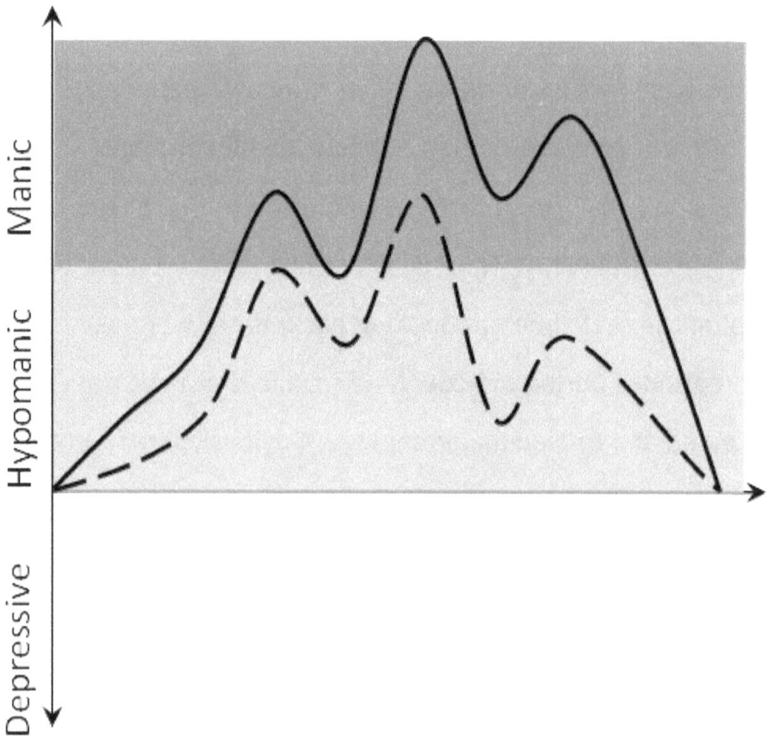

Let's have a quick look at a mixed cycle:

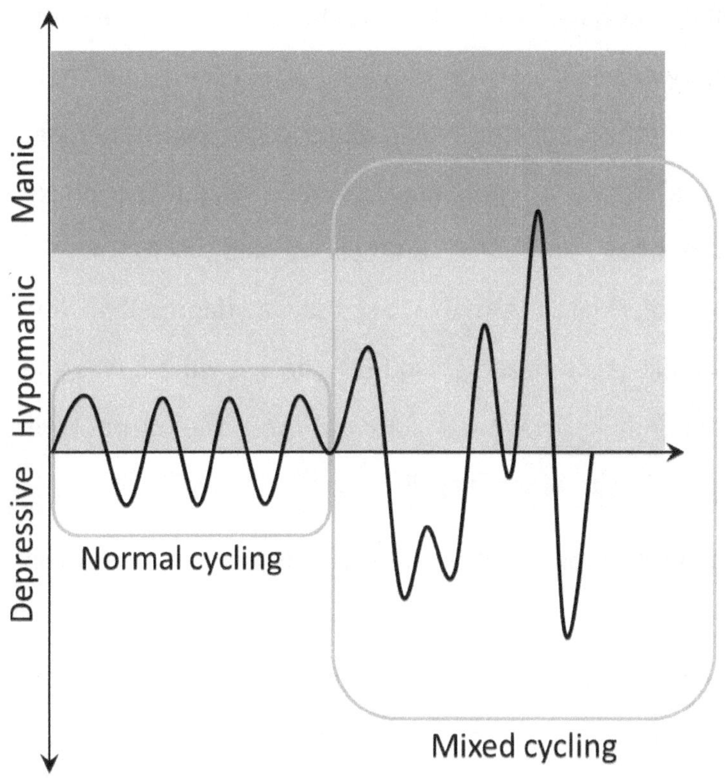

Looking at this diagram it bears saying that the time scale on the graph is short and can even be as short as hours. Here it also becomes useful to understand the wave theory I mentioned earlier. Notice how the frequency of phases shorten and how the amplitudes of the cycles appear to be completely random and unpredictable. This leads to extremely violent mood swings for no apparent reason and subsequent irrational behaviour.

If I may refer back to something I related earlier in the book: When I was going crazy on retail therapy I realise now that I must have had a mixed-manic episode. Do you remember how I said that I bought things to make myself feel better but didn't have an idea or care how I would pay for them? I thought of it later as mania disguised as depression. Now that I understand mixed episodes, I can see what it was and subsequently know what to look out for in the future. I will recognise it when I see it again.

Learning to recognise these little devils is a tricky business and is very likely completely different in your case than it is in mine. I typically detect the warning signs in my sleeping pattern and the intensity of my dreams and the coherency of my speech. The latter is a difficult skill to learn – listening to yourself speaking and understanding whether you are making sense or not.

While manic or hypomanic, it is vitally important that you stay focused on the things you should be doing and not, as best you can, the spur of the moment things. Yes, I know how difficult it is and how doing these things seem so attractive at the time; in fact, they may seem like things demanding immediate attention. I have just one concept here that I need to practice: Self-discipline. It is by no means a skill I have mastered – everything but. There are times that it is among the first things, along with inhibition, that goes out the window, but it is possible to wrestle yourself back into some degree of self-control with arduous effort. It's not impossible, and often your support structure will need to come down on you like a ton of bricks like you, as it is in my case. I may feel that they are raining on my parade, but I have also learnt to trust them, even it is means taking the fun out of things.

Chapter Twelve

Apathy

Another infuriating state in Bipolar is that of apathy. It isn't what can be termed as a *perceived normal* emotional level, but it isn't quite depression either. It is some kind of nether-state. Lately, and at the time of writing this, I've been experiencing a lot of that.

I can basically describe apathy as anger but without the enthusiasm.

What is unpleasant about the state of apathy is that you have just about zero emotional, physical or mental responsiveness. It is the dreaded *Beeeeep* state. It is a bit like being a computer, radically slowing down in the middle of you typing a sentence. You know how and what you are feeling inside, but you find it hard to show or act on your feelings. You do have feelings, but not as intense as with depression when you are mostly just plain sad and down or with hypomania when you are generally ecstatic and on the up.

If I had to guess, that is what happened while I was on Carbamazepine. I doubt that it is directly linked to the medication I take and that it is just another, albeit less frequently discussed mood state of Bipolar.

Apathy spells ill for relationships because of your inability to respond emotionally or physically, which it is also why people often mistake it as depression. This isn't limited to emotional involvement only, but your sex drive drops to an absolute zero. I find myself thinking about sex as much as other men do, which is a lot, but I can't bring myself to act on it while locked down in the state of apathy. This isn't only frustrating to me, but to my wife too. In that lies the problem: You are vaguely aware of your own frustration, but you don't actually feel it on a physical or emotional level. You just exist.

It is very difficult to reason about this while you're in an apathetic state, but I'm doing the best I can. During apathy, just like during depression, your mind feels dull and slowed down, almost like if it is on a low-power standby mode.

I don't find apathetic states to be a prelude or epilogue to any episodes of mania or depression. Sure, you can have a mild depressive episode during such an apathetic state. It has never happened to me, but it also stands to reason that you can also experience a mild, watered-down mania during such a state. It normally returns to the apathetic state, though.

As I am revisiting this piece of writing I find it difficult to add anything to it. Right now, as I am writing this, I am in that neither/nor state which I wouldn't rate as remission, depression or hypomanic either. Standing a couple of paces back from it, I can tell you that it is also one of the least pleasant states of Bipolar and possibly the one I detest the most. It is almost like being in a solid-state – not fluid or gaseous, where you can adapt to a situation and spontaneously take up the available space you would like you normally could. If you are that spontaneous kind of person, that is.

One of the aspects of apathy is avoiding yourself to be committed to anything and I think that it may work from the psychological part backwards to the physiology. It is said and it has been scientifically proven that what you feel or think influences your bodily states. I think that this may be true for the state of apathy. I don't know if all people with Bipolar experience this on a regular basis and what their takes on it are, but these are just my thoughts on it.

Now that I'm revisiting this piece of writing for the umpteenth time, I am still uncertain whether I accurately capture the difference between depression and apathy. Depression, hypomania, and mania are largely *feeling states*, whereas apathy is an unemotional state and a place I, for one, phase out to when I'm feeling threatened in any other state or situations I don't like.

Chapter Thirteen

Borderline

I mentioned earlier, my bouquet of mental illnesses, apart from OCD and anxiety, also include Borderline Personality Disorder. It is often difficult to distinguish the one from the other because they present such similar symptoms.

Let it also be said that Borderline is such a rich topic that it deserves a book by itself.

My diagnosis with Borderline is quite recent, so I am still coming to terms with it and, as with my Bipolar I have the choice of acceptance or denial. In conjunction with Bipolar, it forms quite a nasty combination, especially when the symptoms of the two aren't playing together nicely.

Other than Bipolar which is a clinical condition, Borderline is a personality disorder. That is, purely psychological and ranges in the schizoaffective spectrum of disorders. It is, however, not as simple as going to a psychologist for a couple of sessions and walking out fixed. The only effective treatment for Borderline is said to be Dialectical Behaviour Therapy or DBT for short. DBT focusses mainly on awareness and learning new coping skills. The unfortunate part of it is that DBT is such a new field in psychology and there are very few psychologists practicing it. Unlike Bipolar which constantly influences your moods from the one day to the next because of your varying brain chemistry, Borderline, or in my case at least, would appear to go dormant for unpredictable lengths of time.

There are always Borderline traits present or the remnants thereof, which makes my day-to-day living more complicated with things like anger issues, wrong perspectives of things and difficulties with my own identity and relationships. I am not going to go into the nitty-gritty of Borderline and there are a lot of interesting articles on the Internet on the topic. This book deals mainly with Bipolar and I want to get back to how it influences me.

I mentioned how nasty it gets when their symptoms aren't playing together nicely. When a nasty spell of Borderline wakes up during a depressive, manic or mixed manic cycle, I am in for trouble, or a hard time at the very least. Then I really need to put in a lot of mental effort and the strength I've been harbouring and the knowledge I have into action. Believe me, that is no small feat and I get shaken up really good when it happens.

The difficult part about it is that I need to distinguish or at least control my impulses mentally when my brain chemistry already isn't really helping me. My brain, in whichever state or cycle, is already fighting to curb the effects of my Bipolar and when a nasty spell of Borderline pitches in, well, I basically derail. That's all there is to it. I don't really know how to cope when the two hits me at the same time. My suicide attempts, when you read about it later in the book occurred when the symptoms of my worst Bipolar cycles and Borderline were present at the same time.

Although Borderline is a psychological disorder and can't be treated medically I have found that being on antipsychotics helps to alleviate the symptoms. At least, I find that it is easier to deal with the Borderline while my Bipolar is behaving itself. Borderline symptoms do go into remission and they do not always occur when I cycle. They do, however, recur at random time intervals and if I'm not in a specific severe cycle at the time, it is easier to control the disorder.

I am still to undergo DBT for Borderline although I have been through several Cognitive Behavioural Therapy (CBT) sessions, which barely brought this condition to the front. A lot of what I know about dealing with Borderline I learned from self-help literature on the Internet. Some of it I find more helpful than others. The most important aspect of it I found is awareness. This, I think, is also useful in managing your case of Bipolar.

Here is a little anecdote on the topic of awareness:

A prince was walking one day and found the Buddha sitting under a tree. He asked him what it is that he and his monks do. The Buddha answered him that they eat, they walk and breathe. The prince then said that these were the same things everybody does. The Buddha replied that they did so with awareness – that they were really drinking in what they did.

As I am typing this, I am aware that, owing to my oily skin, the keys under my fingers feel slightly slippery, my palms are feeling sweaty, that I'm feeling the ambient heat and humidity, and that my left ear is itching. There is no skill in that, however. The skill comes in where you must be aware of what, or how you feel what you feel. How does anger feel like to you? And joy? Then, how do you respond to those feelings? Are your responses rational and are they proportional?

That balance between *rational* and *proportional* trips me up a lot of the time. If I feel angry towards someone or a situation, there is occasionally no real reason for it. I overreact a lot of the time, meaning that my responses may not always be proportional.

Finding some sort of golden midway is virtually impossible with Borderline – just about everything is either black or white. Try coping with that when you are experiencing a major episode. I'm not saying that it is impossible, but it does require a great feat of mental and personal strength.

Chapter Fourteen

Remission

If you have Bipolar, remission is the place you want to be at. It takes hard work from yourself and your caregivers to get and keep you there. It is the result of a long period of treatment with the correct medication, therapy, and care.

Remission is when your symptoms, for want of a better description, go away. You can function like how I perceive to be, a *normal* person does. Your emotional responses are rational, and your trains of thought are logical, untainted by the distortions that depressive or manic states my put on it. You can pick up on the tune of your life and keep singing to the correct words without making new words up to try to fit the melody.

Many people with Bipolar, unfortunately, believe that they are cured of Bipolar when they go into remission and stop taking their medication. Learn from my experience that this is a bad move. Always remember that Bipolar is a life-long condition which is at the best of times under control, but never cured. To date, there is no cure for Bipolar.

Remission is my obviously favourite state of having Bipolar, mainly because I know how I am going to feel or be able to predict at least what my emotional responses to environmental triggers will be. It is not a guessing game or an emotional roller coaster ride. You actually have grips on how you feel and when you feel it and to what degree.

People can actually, in my own opinion, live with you and I can live with myself cosily. I don't see a clown, a monster or a pathetic mess when I look in the mirror. I can live with myself in peace. You can actually get to know who you really are like I did once I went into remission, perhaps for the first time in my life.

Remission isn't without its disadvantages. There isn't the same energy as with a manic or hypomanic phase, which is a small trade-off for the other advantages of remission. The real downside of remission to me is to know that sooner or later, but hopefully later, there is going to be a relapse. It is like a sword hanging over my head daily. It is a fear, almost a phobia when I am in remission, but being of a sounder mind, I can deal with that fear.

While in remission I think it wise to think about my life: Where I've been, where I'm going to. I do this when I can think clearly about things. I make a point of not thinking about my life too much while overly depressed or hypomanic. I also refrain from making life-changing decisions during such times. My degree of success is, of course, limited by the intensity of the specific episode. The intensity always influences the quality of the decision made.

In remission, you can afford to indulge, but not overindulge in the things you enjoy. Remember, you want to be in remission as long as you can, so it is up to you to do things right if you want to stay in remission. I take it easy especially with alcohol (which I generally avoid altogether now,) the comfort food, because yes, things actually taste and smell better to me when I am in remission. But in moderation – some medications for Bipolar may be conducive to weight gain.

The other great part about remission is that my sex drive returns to normal. I don't get manic too often and many people with Bipolar have reported that they experience heightened sex drive, if not complete insatiability during mania. I wouldn't know, because as I have stated earlier, my manias are coupled with no small degree of feelings of shame. In depression and apathy, I can forget about sexual arousal. So, when in remission I feel like I could return to having a normal sex life.

Remission doesn't only encapsulate the things I stated above. It isn't the nether-state one gets used to when one has that solid-state apathy. I would venture as far to say that you are the likeable person you are meant to be – you'll notice that people respond to you in a better way, or in a way you expect them to at least. You don't get treated as the "bird with a broken wing," to borrow the expression from Mom; because while in remission you can show others how to fly; not the lopsided flight you have during mania or hypomania, but how it is really meant to be.

During remission, you can enjoy life to the fullest and unlike me, you don't need to fear the sword of relapse hanging over you. Surely, it will come down on you sooner or later and you need to be prepared for that. Have an action plan in place.

What do I mean by an action plan? I am very open with my wife and the moment I feel that I may be cycling I tell her so. I may not know which way I might cycle, but it will almost always be to the depressive side.

However, let this not keep you from enjoying remission but just this word of caution: Like any phase in Bipolar, it doesn't last. Therefore, keep your eyes and ears and heart open. Listen to what your body is telling you once you know what to look for. Also, listen to your caregivers – they may be the best early detection system you may have in place.

But if you made it to remission – well done to you and on your circle of caregivers. I wish you a long and happy stay.

Chapter Fifteen

How I experience emotions and deal, or don't deal, with them

People with Bipolar like me tend to experience emotions in the superlative degree. Whether we get sad, happy, jolly, angry or whatever, it is normally greatly so.

I'd like to write about anger a bit. I have a particularly nasty anger, and it scares even me when it comes out. I may have mentioned that I'm not the biggest of guys, but when I get angry, big guys stay out of my way. If I believed in auras and people who claim to be able to read them I would have accepted it if they told me that my aura turns pitch black when I get angry. My heart rate doubles, my face and neck flush bright red, my eyes flash fire and I literally shake.

The reason for writing about it is that I often get angry like that, and you guessed it, it isn't there one moment and gone the next. It often lingers for quite some time. But it also often happens that I get that fleeting fit of rage, which is common in people with Bipolar. This often gets worse: Sometimes it is a day-long affair, sometimes even longer. In these cases it is just better, and safer, to stay out of harm's way.

On days like these, I find it best to isolate myself as best as I can for the sake of my family. I know it is often hurtful especially to the children because I can't offer them an explanation they will understand. *"Daddy isn't feeling well,"* or *"Daddy has a bad headache,"* has to suffice. I get so sick of feeding them these half-truths. But then, how can I explain it to them in a way that they would understand? *"Daddy is very angry for no reason today and doesn't want to say or do things to upset you."*

I learnt something about anger a while back though. Anger is a go-to emotion for me. There are a lot of things that can make me angry, so anger is not the root, it's the fruit. I have a lot of underlying feelings of shame – something I recently discovered in therapy. It is easier to get angry about whatever happened that makes me experience that shame than to feel ashamed.

Being a go-to, I think of anger as a super-highway. There are many places, or triggering emotions, where things can hop onto the anger highway. The problem with that highway is that there is often no way of knowing where it leads to and it may hop off at at completely different emotion.

To use an example: I am impatient. So I get angry about whatever is causing my impatience instead of dealing with it, often because I feel incapable of doing so. So, it gets onto the anger highway at the interchange and races in some direction and hops off at another interchange to a different emotion like guilt – because you got angry. Or from guilt, it may hop onto the highway and get off it again at shame. If you can identify with this, I think that it may be a good idea to sketch yourself a diagram of your highway – mine was quite enlightening. Then find and implement measures to keep whatever emotions that *used to* get you on the anger highway off it.

A cup of coffee is an essential part of my functioning and I will go to the kitchen for a cuppa and find a mess on the floor. Then the *"Whodunit, and why wasn't it cleaned up?"* drives me up the wall. Why does the other one just look at the mess and ignore it? And before you know it, *kaboom!* I explode, splashing absolutely everyone around me, guilty or not, with the super-heated water of anger and frustration inside of me.

The question I'm always asking myself is this: Would I have reacted this way if I didn't have Bipolar, or at least if I was a little more stable at the time? The conclusion I come to is that I'd probably still have been angry because there was a violation of a principle. Yet, how many of my own principles did I violate when I exploded? Furthermore, I think that the intensity could be turned down by a thousand degrees or so if I obeyed my principles at the time.

Or could I walk with a cowbell around my neck on a day like that and have people clear the area when they hear the sound of me approaching?

Unfortunately, we live in an angry little world and there are more things that drive us gaga than there are things to help us discharge our tense emotional states. This is true for all people: There is no sure-fire way to get rid of anger. People who tell you so are trying to sell you a book as I am trying to do, a punching bag or counselling. We all have to find what works for us: In my case, isolation, putting on headphones with some really loud music on works – heavy stuff like Beethoven, Rachmaninov, Bach, Rammstein or Metallica. It doesn't really calm me down, but it does seem to make it more bearable, hearing that there are those who understand what I feel. It takes a bit of the edge off and if it is loud enough, it actually trumps the angry Voices in my head. This therapy doesn't always work though, especially not when I get really bad anxiety attacks as I sometimes do. Then I try to reduce sensory triggers to an absolute minimum.

My anger is usually intense and irrational. People often talk of jealousy as the green monster. My anger is a big, ugly, red monster and when let loose, tramples everything in its path and is indeed very hard to get a leash on. So, before it grows too big, I keep it in a cage. I make a conscious effort not to get angry – it may be a decision, which gets easier with self-discipline and practice. The trick to this approach is something I am yet to master, and that is not to bottle or internalise that anger because sooner or later it will bite you in the ass.

I guess that when you have Bipolar, many things must become mind over matter somehow. Once we really and truly get a hold of ourselves I jokingly think that we have more resolve and reach a higher level of enlightenment. Just remember that *"get over yourself"* isn't something you should *ever* say to yourself or to someone with Bipolar, because it is insensitive and stigmatises the condition to the person by making them feel inferior to you.

Do I really deal with my anger issues? I think I have come a long way with it since breaking my finger when punching my brother at the tender age of eleven years old.

To cite another example of my anger getting the better of me – not too long ago my daughter posted something on

Facebook which, in my opinion, was a real insult to her mother. Did I explode! The problem with these outbursts are often not what we say, but how we say them. The content of what I told her would have more or less been the same, but I would have done well to tone it down a hundred degrees or so.

Was this directly related to me having Bipolar? No, I don't think so.

Did I learn something from this? Yes. I am saying this again, but Bipolar is not always an excuse for your reactions and secondly, as a parent with Bipolar you need to think twice before you act. To paraphrase the Holy Bible – you need not only one, but two guards for your mouth.

The list of emotions I deal with on almost a daily basis is a long one. There is, apart from anger and rage, ecstasy and joy, trust and acceptance, fear and terror, surprise and distraction, sadness and pensiveness, boredom and disgust. These, apart from anger, are not my most predominant emotional states; it is purely illustrative.

Ecstasy and joy are easy to deal with – people who have issues with these emotions are in serious need of help. The problem with joy and ecstasy though, is that the superlative of joy in a manic or hypomanic phase can be dangerous to me because it is then that I start doing crazy things like maxing out credit cards and do softball slides in the parking lot. On dealing with it? I'm not sure that I've completely dealt with it in the regard that I have become a rather blunt person and sadly avoid what most of my peers may consider fun. It takes a lot to get me excited these days, apart from every 1,000 words I write in this book, which really excites me. A psychologist pointed it out to me the other day that I like playing aloof, starting with my facial expression. I taught myself to keep my facial expression neutral at all times because it affords me the luxury of people not knowing what I am thinking or feeling, and therein is an amazing and powerful comfort zone. Besides, if people knew what I thought, I'd get punched in the face quite often.

I have trust issues with people and things and on some days it boils right down to the level of paranoia. That is what you get when fear and mistrust get combined. I often feel paranoia, even though sometimes I think it can be substantiated. I have been scared of getting hijacked. I knew that it was a real risk in my case since I used to travel to work so early in the mornings and I drove through some dodgy areas. The level of fear exceeded the level of reason and I constantly had to remind myself that I have driven the same route a thousand times over and never, not even once, observed anything that closely resembled a potential hijacker or a hijacking situation.

While I'm on the topic of trust issues with people: Initially, I implicitly trusted people and to a certain degree and I still do, depending on my first impression of a person. But I have been disappointed once too often and trust is a hard-earned commodity in my books. Why do I find trust so important? Well, who doesn't? I am a person who wears his heart on his sleeve and I don't see it ever-changing. I really put myself out there, even in this book. This increases my chances of being hurt by people. I think of myself as a bit of an emotional and mental exhibitionist. I don't keep many secrets from people; in fact, I make it my business to try and have none because secrets are things that turn around and bite you in the ass.

What I find hurtful and breaks my trust in people is dishonesty. I am honest toward people and want them to extend the same courtesy to me. How do I feel when my trust is betrayed? Obviously, I will feel sad and disappointed, even to the point of anger and depression sometimes. However, I have learnt to take a breach like a little slap on the cheek because my trust has been betrayed enough times for me to know that most people I met weren't trustworthy. I don't know if you have had better experiences than I did and if I am just the unlucky one. You have to bend over backward quite a bit to earn my trust sometimes and it doesn't bother me in the slightest. Trust issue dealt with. To my own satisfaction, anyway.

A while back one of my children lost all of the trust I had in them. It was extremely hurtful coming from one of my own. We always believe the best in people, especially our children, and I'm certain that with time that trust will grow back to what it was, but it will forever be tarnished by a scar. So it is with other people – trust is a precious commodity I'll issue you with, free of charge, but be damn careful what you do with it. What I find really sad is that the trust gained again is being tested now. I need to get into a state of mental and emotional preparedness for it because like the first time, this will hit me really hard if not harder. A punch on scar tissue is more painful than a punch on other flesh.

Then: fear and terror. Nasty words, aren't they? I think that they are especially so if you have Bipolar. My fears and terrors are gripping and debilitating and once again it comes back to paranoia for me. Let's take an example: In my younger days, I've been terrified of the dark and whatever may be lurking in it. I that that specific fear of the dark isn't an abnormal thing in children, but I couldn't sleep without my Pinocchio night light on, the one I got for Christmas when I was four years old. I still remember waking up in the middle of the night, switching it off and going to my parent's bedroom to sleep with them simply because even the night light wasn't effective enough in my books. That's how terrified I was of the dark and it was a fear that lasted deep into my teens. I wouldn't say that darkness no longer makes me feel queasy, but I'm no longer afraid of it.

There are still things that can completely freak me out, but I will not be discussing them in this book. I think that it all comes back to fight or flight. There is another state in there not many people considered and that is *freeze*. I tend to freeze. That means that I find myself freezing in an unknown situation I haven't yet contemplated or foreseen. I find myself incapable of acting on the trigger, often resulting in more harm than had I chosen fight or flight. I often find it hard to assess and act sometimes a situation and act. Here is another idea for you that worked for me: Contemplate situations and your subsequent reactions to them. It is called being proactive and I found that it helped me a lot, albeit a kind of programmed response.

Another example of what I fear, which lasts to this day, is noise. I get panicky – even aggressive – in noisy environments especially when crowds are involved like at busy shopping malls. This, contrary to my fear of darkness, is perpetually growing worse as I age. Enough noise in an unfamiliar environment can set off an anxiety attack which means that it is time for a quick dose of Clobazam and evasive action. It doesn't take the anxiety attack away but makes it more bearable.

So how do I deal with it? Simply by avoiding the trigger as best I can. Also, if I can anticipate it, I can take my Clobazam in advance. I can't as I did with darkness really substantiate that fear, apart maybe that it was part of my upbringing. I don't understand why, because the fear of darkness was laid aside when I realised that none of the things I feared dwelled in darkness has come out to harm me.

I tend to be distractible and my students knew it. They also exploited it on a day they don't feel like working. It was easy for me to be pulled off onto a tangent to what I'm doing, even now. Not that I find concentration difficult or have

ADHD, simply for the reasons that my mind can be extremely busy at times and not follow the main track of thought, or it simply derails from time to time. I have learned how to, to a certain degree, consciously discipline my mind to keep focus. The success rate on this varies from time to time of course. It all depends on my mood phase. When I am feeling depressed, I am only capable of short bursts of concentration but when manic, they can either be longer, or completely absent. It often amazes me how much or how little one can accomplish while in a manic or hypomanic phase.

The range of emotions that humans experience is a book by itself – that is what made people like Freud, Jung and their peers so famous. They could name and classify them. Unfortunately, I'm not that smart and I can only superficially touch on my predominant ones. Yours will in all probability be different from mine – that's why you may need a psychologist, to help you make sense of what you feel.

As I stated earlier in this chapter, my predominant emotion or state is anger in its many forms. Because I know now what the origins of my anger are, I can deal with it and I do that on a daily basis. For almost every reaction I have, I have to ask myself if it is the angry little man speaking again? Is it the perpetual pessimist who sees problems where none exist?

That is my reality. These are the cognitive emotions I struggle with on a daily basis. And I don't always win.

There is as far as can tell, no comprehensive self-help literature on Bipolar, or none that I've encountered or can recommend apart from brochures of organisations like SADAG, which are available to download free of charge from their website. I do urge you to look at the *further reading* part of this book as I cite some really useful technical resources. If you remember that I pointed it out, everyone's case of Bipolar is so unique and anything, including what I am saying is mostly generic, or true in my case anyway.

Primarily, beyond a healthy measure of discipline, I'm kind to myself. I can't always predict how I will feel about a stimulus, but I can choose how I react to it. I have said before that I have some programmed responses, which isn't a bad thing. The down-side to it though is that it takes away spontaneity from my life and for a great part of my life I feel like I'm living like a robot and generally have a poorer quality of life. It doesn't have to be true for you, though.

I mostly keep my emotions are suppressed, or at least I hide them rather well – I could have been a good poker player if I could bluff but I'm no good at that. Still, I haven't answered the full question about how I help myself. Yes, kindness is important but so is self-discipline. The tricky part which I fail miserably at most of the time is the kindness part. I know what happens when I am too kind to myself. But then again, I am constantly flogging myself for the slightest thing I step out of order.

I like finding a balance between alone time and time I spend with people. Both of these interactions are important to me: Spending time with myself enables me to investigate my thoughts and feelings while spending time with others help me place things in perspective and serves as fresh stimuli. No person is an island, not even us ones with Bipolar.

Here are some things that help me cope with my Bipolar emotions and actions; maybe there is be something useful to you in here too.

Breathe. I make a conscious effort of breathing deeply at least once a day. Apart from increasing the flow of oxygen to the brain, it is very relaxing. I especially take deep breaths when I realise that I am getting anxious, or as deep as my body would allow me – anxiety goes coupled with short breaths.

Have a hobby other than watching TV or movies – create something. Paint. Draw. Write poetry. Go SCUBA diving. Learn a new language. TV and movies generally suppress activity in the frontal lobe of the brain – that is where your active thought happens, and decisions are formulated. A sad movie may make me slip into a depression, whereas I have seen movies that are visually so overwhelming in movement, colour and sound that it tipped me into mania. All of that only from watching movies. Personally, I like seeing something that appears messy to become tidy again. Also, the steady drone of the lawnmower creates a blissful emptiness in my head. I love that *mindlessness.*

I listen to a lot of music. The genre will depend on my mood. I have music I listen to when depressed and music I listen to when manic or hypomanic. The choices I make therein may surprise you – when I'm feeling manic or hypomanic I choose to listen to heavier classical music because it stimulates a calmer brainwave. I think they are called beta waves. When depressed I listen to heavier rock and metal – it feels to me that the artists understand how I feel and by relating to them it makes me feel better because

I feel that I'm not alone and that realisation gives me a lift. Music always understands.

From time to time, I clean the house myself and get rid of what I perceive to be junk. Getting the dust off the shelves and the dirt off the floor is good for me because it becomes a metaphor for doing the same with my soul. I can't say that this is an enjoyable task, but if there is no-one around the house and it's just me and my music, I often enjoy it.

A lot of literature has lately been written on the topic of emotional care animals. If you'll swear to me to take good care of it, get a dog. Dogs are indeed man's best friend. A dog will always give you unconditional love, even if you do not want to give it to yourself. You can even have a conversation with your dog – they are incredibly good listeners and they don't keep interrupting you. In my own case, how I feel towards my dog is also a good barometer of my emotional state. Please note that I say how I feel, not how I act. Always act with loving-kindness towards your dog – they give you their best and deserve your best in return.

Finally, I write. Paper is patient and it always listens to what you have to say. I can express myself on a sheet of paper better than I can verbally. If I'm feeling agitated I can cuss and swear all I want or write a poem or essay and burn it afterwards. The same is true with melancholy and sadness, joy and elation. Paper is a wonderful thing and the pen is indeed mightier than the sword.

PART FOUR

WHAT YOU NEED TO KNOW

Chapter Sixteen

If you have Bipolar

The initial diagnosis of Bipolar may initially seem like a terrible thing, mostly because it is. However, if I were to wager a bet, I'd say that you knew all along that something wasn't right before you were diagnosed. You knew that something big and something serious was wrong with you. You have probably seen how some, even petty, things make you feel crazy, seem crazy and act crazy.

I am writing this chapter based on the premise that you have decided to accept your condition – if you haven't, don't stop reading now, please. There may still be valuable information for you in this chapter. I may also repeat myself on a couple of issues I have stated in the book so far because I think they bear reiteration.

The diagnosis of Bipolar may come as a relief to some as I have seen it happen but also remember that it may come as a partial shock as it was in my own case. It may also come as a complete shock to you as if being hit directly on your solar plexus. The fact of the matter remains, and it is this: Once you are diagnosed with Bipolar your problem, your demon, call it what you will, has a name. If it has been identified and named, it can be fought.

As you walk down the road of Bipolar you should in time find peace with it. If you don't, you may get a second and a third opinion from different psychiatrists or may need further CBT to help you accept the fact that the diagnosis of Bipolar has been confirmed to you. All the while I need you to remember that just because you have been diagnosed with a mental illness doesn't make you a bad person. It doesn't make you an inferior human being or a cracked nut.

I pointed out this fact earlier, but it may be worth mentioning again: People who have Bipolar are more often depressed than not. Manias and hypomanias are relatively quite rare actually. You may, however, like it was with me, be stuck in a lingering mania or hypomania, lasting for months. Depression is many times more likely to occur than mania or hypomania with people with Bipolar.

It was once said that living with Bipolar or major depression is akin to living in a body where your brain is trying its level best to kill the body you live in. You are therefore prone to suicide ideation if you don't know it yet. Even worse, you may become suicidally depressed. It was like that with me in more than one case. There will be times when suicide will seem nothing short of a sweet release to you. There are some days when it may seem like the only way out to you but if there is something you should know about Bipolar, it is that nothing of what you feel is permanent. It is going to change sooner or later, whether it is depression, mania or hypomania. You are fortunately or unfortunately stuck on that roller-coaster with its ever-continuing ups and downs and no stop.

On the topic of mania or hypomania: I have also contemplated suicide during mania or hypomania too, simply because of that dreaded *coming down* drop at the end of the episode. It has value to mention that coming down from mania or hypomania doesn't always lead to depression.

What I am driving towards is that during some point you are most likely be bound to have suicidal thoughts, if not ideation. I'm not going to be the one to give you the lecture about what it will do to those you leave behind. I believe that you are mentally capable of working that out for yourself. More often than not people with Bipolar are extraordinarily intellectually gifted people.

As a person with Bipolar, you are most probably bound to have psychological or social issues. You will more likely than not at some stage end up in a psychologist's consulting room. There is no shame in that. Consider that in the United States only 2.6% of the national population are afflicted with Bipolar disorder. Do you honestly think that in a country with approximately 34 psychologists per 100,000 people, psychologists earn their rather comfortable livings from people with Bipolar only?

The reason you are likely to end up with a psychologist or therapist of sorts is that we people with Bipolar or other mental illnesses for that matter have a harder time working through our issues. Part of it as I mentioned, are trust issues. We don't just talk to people and I believe that trust is as I said earlier, a hard-earned commodity from a person with any mental illness and that it is always in a sensitive balance. I am not saying that if you have Bipolar that you have to see a psychologist too; I just found it to be helpful at times. A psychologist is bound by law and by ethic not to discuss anything you share with them and what you share remains within the walls of their consulting rooms. The same cannot be said when you discuss things with friends. Gossip is a nasty thing and even your friends are people with feet of clay. Keep your issues within the closed circle of your caregivers of which your psychologist or therapist can be a part.

While I'm on the topic of caregivers, let's talk about that for a bit. I already said that your caregivers need to be people you feel comfortable with and whom you know you can trust. Your primary caregiver won't be your psychiatrist or psychologist. It will be an ordinary person closest to you like a spouse, partner or parent. It should be a person who knows you inside and out, someone who can give you an *outside looking in* perspective. It should be a person who you don't want to hide your feelings from. You may want to hide the intensity of those feelings and emotions, but not the feeling and emotion themselves. From my own experience I can tell you that there were times I was livid with my wife and all I let her on to is that I was angry, although I think she rubbed the pennies together and knew.

Obviously, there needs to be a strong personal bond between you and your primary caregiver. The effects of this bond failing will be as devastating to you as it was to me when my marriage failed. Primary caregivers are usually exceptionally strong, trustworthy and compassionate people but don't latch onto a person as a primary caregiver just because they possess these qualities. Don't forget to thank them from time to time or to express your appreciation towards them. Being the primary caregiver to a person with Bipolar is certainly no walk in the park.

The next important person, if not the second most important after your primary caregiver, is a psychiatrist who has the unenviable task of correctly medicating you. Accept that the process of correctly medicating you is exactly that: A process of trial and error. Finding your personal *cocktail* of medications is no small task. If you are very lucky it may happen over a matter of days or weeks, or it may take months. Your psychiatrist should be a person you feel comfortable with. I finally found a psychiatrist I'm completely comfortable with four years into my diagnosis. Your psychiatrist is also someone who will be asking you how you feel emotionally and physically, and these questions may often feel intrusive to you. They have to take what you say, observe your body language and make clinical sense of it. I honestly don't have experience of many psychiatrists but from the ratio of my own experience, good psychiatrists aren't two a penny. Inherently, your psychiatrist is someone you trust with your life. You might as well find one you trust and like. For the clinical part, they are the ones who prevent your brain from killing your body.

In my own case, my caregivers are a closed circle of people. I want to include my parents in it though because for a long time, especially after my initial diagnosis, they were just about my only caregivers. This is giving them the kudos they deserve. Remember how I refused to see a psychiatrist? Remember how I stated that they were the ones who helped me pick up the pieces after my divorce and how you can throw the worst things at people? To some extent, they are still part of that circle. They have gone to extraordinary lengths to understand my condition and still offer me sound advice from time to time. Since they are not my primary caregivers anymore, they don't always see the full picture mostly because I have moved on, and now have my wonderful wife as my primary caregiver.

I can ramble on forever about the effects of Bipolar and how it influences your daily life, and if you would want to come over for a braai, we could talk about it all at length. I do however urge you to refer to the *further reading* section of this book – I cite some good resources in there.

Now that that has been said, let's talk about the matter of you managing your condition. Bipolar, like any other chronic illness, requires management. High or low blood pressure demands chronic treatment but so does Bipolar, and it doesn't only require popping pills.

Here is the part you may not want to hear: You will be taking medication for the rest of your life if you have Bipolar and you plan to manage it. This is probably, or in my case at least, the single most important aspect of managing my illness. I had a very hard time coming to terms with this fact because I believed that taking pills was for old or sick people. The hard realisation you have to come to is that you *are* ill, and seriously so. These are harsh words to hear but whether you like it or not, that is the case. Bipolar comes in varying degrees of intensities and you may not have it that bad. Still, the long and short of it is that you do require medication. If you choose not to take your medication is it is to your own detriment, as it was in my case. You may by chance be luckier than me, but I wouldn't stake a wager on it. I have heard of people who stopped taking their medication as an act of faith, and although I don't doubt the Creator's ability to heal you, it didn't turn out too well for them. It is a chance I refuse to take – the Creator also created people to help you. And whether you want to hear this or not, I believe that there is a divine purpose to you being here.

Trust, utilise and respect your support structure. Be upfront about your feelings with your primary caregiver. Visit your psychiatrist as regularly as they recommend. I see my psychiatrist once in three months on her recommendation, or in case of emergency and experience has taught me to trust her on that, simply because my specific case of Bipolar is such a shapeshifter. If you have a hard time dealing with an emotional issue, call in the help of your psychologist or therapist; that is what they are there for.

You have a responsibility toward your caregivers too and that lies in not abusing them. What do I mean by abuse? As for your primary caregiver, go figure. They are probably the person closest to you and you have the power to cause them terrible pain. As for the other stakeholders in your group of caregivers, they are there to help you. Allow them to do their jobs.

Know your triggers and avoid them as best you could. As I have pointed out, I am afraid of crowds and noise. I can't always avoid them due to the very nature of life. I can, however, take Clobazam when I foresee the situation coming up. Another dangerous trigger to me is alcohol, which I can avoid altogether. If you don't know it yet, take it from me that you don't need alcohol to enjoy yourself. I pointed out earlier that you may want to keep a mood journal to help you identify your triggers.

Maintain a healthy sleeping pattern or as my psychiatrist says, maintain good sleep hygiene. Look that up on Google – it is very useful information and like me, you may discover that you have had the wrong approach to sleep all your life. Find out how much sleep you need. You will notice that when you are in a manic or hypomanic phase it feels like you can do with less sleep and feel like you need more sleep during a depression. Try to maintain the same number of hours. If you need to, let your general practitioner or psychiatrist prescribe suitable sleeping tablets to you, but remember my golden rule of thumb: Don't put any CNS acting medication into your body without consulting with a medical professional who knows about your condition and what medications you take for it.

Finally, knowledge is power. Find out as much as you can about Bipolar. This book is only a small step in that direction and I can only hope that you are finding it useful. The more you know about Bipolar and other people's experiences with it, the better you will be equipped in dealing with your own case. There are a lot of impossible variables in Bipolar but also many constants. Learn what you can and apply that knowledge. There is no reason to make the same mistakes other people or I made, but you can have my assurances that you will make those same mistakes from time to time. I still read, listen and learn every day.

These things I pointed out are not the alpha and omega of managing your condition. There may be things that apply to you that I have not pointed out here, but I think that these are good points of departure. Find out what needs to be fixed in your own condition of Bipolar and remedy it. What *I* want at the end of the day is a stable, fulfilling and productive life and these are the measures I have to implement to have that.

In the end, when all is said and done, that means that I alone have to accept responsibility for myself and my own life. If you plan to have the same, you should do the same. Your caregivers can only do so much for you, but their best efforts will be in vain if you just sit down and wait for them to make things happen for you. That's not how it works.

Sooner, rather than later, you will have to accept the ultimate responsibility for your own well-being and the management of your illness. There are no magic tricks when it comes to managing and living with Bipolar, and nobody ever said that it will be easy. That's where the strength of character comes in. Nobody was born to be a loser. If you believe that you are a loser, I need you to change that belief *now*. If you believe that you are a waste of space, change that belief *now*. If you feel sorry for yourself for having Bipolar on some days, that's OK. So do I – I will admit that I even feel sorry for myself for two or three days running. However, you can't stay sorry for yourself forever if you plan to lead a productive life with Bipolar.

In this chapter, I am by no means implying that I have the art of living with Bipolar down to a tee. In fact, I should practice what I preach here all the time, not only when it suits me. This is just what I consider to be good advice from the angle I see it and my own meandering experience. If I said it once, I've said it a million times: Your case of Bipolar will present differently from mine, but the underlying principles are still the same.

So, get out there and *live!*

Chapter Seventeen

Help! Someone I know may have Bipolar!

This chapter is more intended for those living with a person they may suspect to have Bipolar. If you already have a diagnosis for the person or are suffering from Bipolar yourself, you can skip over this chapter. It does contain some useful information though, just in case you were interested.

Let's get this straight right from the beginning: You don't just think that because someone is moody they have Bipolar. My daughter told me the other day of her teacher who is moody and appears to behave erratically from time to time. Her friends then joke on the playgrounds that the teacher must have Bipolar. This little anecdote makes me realise a couple of things:

Firstly, Bipolar has become such a popular diagnosis and is blown out of proportion to such an extent by mass media that even your average teenager thinks that they know what it's about. Secondly, every Tom, Dick and Harry thinks they are qualified to diagnose the illness. Thirdly, people seem to think that Bipolar is some kind of joke and subsequently, even among people as young as teenagers, Bipolar is already stigmatised. As it turns out, this teacher has a mentally retarded son, which causes her high levels of stress.

In a similar story, I was recently told a pupil's one teacher was also constantly, for want of a better word, bitchy with her class. She was constantly punishing them, yelling at them and giving them lots of homework. As it turned out her husband had recently passed away and she was dealing with her grief in that way because she didn't know any better. Obviously, the lady had more of a depressive spell or disorder and each person may just handle such trauma differently. I shudder to think of what that poor teacher must have been called on the playgrounds even though she was only a primary school teacher. Kids these days!

This book is partially intended to make the life of those living with a person with Bipolar easier or at least provide some tools or strategies to deal with it. But what do you do while you only suspect the illness? I already stated this, but Bipolar disorder is definitely not the be-all and end-all of psychiatric illnesses. I'm not discussing all these other illnesses; I am going to try and limit it to Bipolar.

I will cut back to the chase just now.

I have talked a lot about some of the ins and outs of Bipolar in this book. This should give you enough information to give you at least a clue to suspect that someone you know may have Bipolar. The question is what do you stand to do about it. The following is from my own experience and how I think it should be done, and once again, is not absolute.

If the person doesn't already know it, you will need to help the person realise that something isn't right and that they may need professional help. Good luck with that part. Don't dally around with people who aren't really close to you – I'm thinking spouses, partners, and direct family members here and maybe the closest of close friends too, but no closer than that. If you suspect that a colleague or someone else you have dealings with may be affected, I suggest you follow company protocols for that. Many companies these days have departments looking out for the social wellbeing of their employees. Many people may argue that you should leave a case like that alone, but not me. Nobody should suffer and cause others to suffer with them when an illness like Bipolar may be present. If you saw someone suffering and you were in the position to help them, you would sound the alarm at the very least. That is basic humanity. Wouldn't you expect that someone did the same for you if the roles were reversed?

It may be useful to use the information contained in this book as a barometer and monitor to a person's erratic behaviour to some degree. Breaking your observations to that person is a whole different ballgame. People don't like to hear that there may be something wrong with them, especially if you think it may be a mental health problem. Hearing someone close to you think that you are mentally unstable, let alone ill, is something that may sink a relationship altogether. The only way to navigate a rugged mountain is to go over it, and if you are in that position with such a person that is exactly where you find yourself: A treacherous, rugged mountain.

General practitioners are useful in the initial diagnosis and may, based on their observations refer a patient to a psychiatrist. It may be quite easy to convince a depressed person to go to a general practitioner to get help. The general practitioner is qualified to make the appropriate observations and make the referral. This is perhaps the easiest and safest of routes to consider if you're afraid of the other options. Just know that a person in a lingering mania will most probably not fall for this trick.

Another way to take care of the problem is to give the person some information to read through, maybe even this book if you find it to be useful. They may just be able to pick up that some of the traits I relate also applies to them to some degree. There are also many shorter information pieces available which may be obtainable free of charge through your general practitioner or on the Internet – I read up about my symptoms on the Internet, so I already had my suspicions by the time I was bullied into finding help.

If you wish to approach it in a more personal way, I suggest that you sit the person down and point out some of your observations, but don't just throw your experiences and your feelings at them. Keep calm, speak in a soft and caring tone and stick to the facts. Ask the person if they have noticed some irregularities in their behaviour. Don't go in unarmed: Have some examples at the ready as to when you may believe that the person may have acted completely out of character. Better still would be if you can have examples about cases where the person reacted one way and in the others completely and erratically and out of character in the same kind of situation. If the person observed these irregularities and are asking themselves why they acted that way too, that's great. That is the golden opportunity you are looking for to suggest to the person that maybe they can go and see a psychologist; remember, my route was psychologist first and psychiatrist second.

On the other hand, you may also be dealing with a person as stubborn as me which makes it a whole lot more difficult. In my own case, it turned out to be people teaming up against me, eventually causing me to budge. That is foul play, but sometimes it is the only available option and should not be thrown out as an option. This opposing team consisted of my ex and my parents and maybe one or two more stakeholders. I can't quite remember because I was maybe just a little deranged at the time. However, with enough reason, persuasion or nudging can get through to a person in the end.

There may be several more strategies to deal with this most difficult and tricky of situations. Some are more delicate than some others, but some may also be akin to bulldozing a person if you're in the position to do so, like when you are a parent of someone younger than eighteen years of age. Once again, remember that you do not want to lose your loved one's trust or sink the relationship, because chances are that you will end up in their caregiver group. You know the person and in the end, it is your unenviable task to decide how to approach the matter with them.

Okay, let's assume that the hard part is over now: You have convinced the person in question that they may need help and they may have returned with some kind of diagnosis. It may even happen that while a person is being diagnosed for the first time, they may be hospitalised while the diagnosis is being made as I have seen it happen. I have seen this happen more than once but the essence here is that the person not only knows but feels that they have your support, trust, and empathy. Hearing that you have any kind of mental disorder is no laughing matter. Visit them in the hospital and take them their favourite treats, but above all, give them your time. Always remember that by giving someone some of your time, irrespective of the circumstances, you give them something you can never have back, which counts among the greatest gifts you can give.

Now you need to educate *yourself* on their condition. There are so many resources available on the Internet, but also refer to the *further reading* section of this book. I list some excellent resources there. You need to be able to apply the knowledge you gather, including the information in this book, and apply it to the specific person. Remember that any advice that can be offered in dealing with mental illness, including that in this book, is generic. Each person's case is as unique as the person's personality. You don't need to become an expert on the topic of Bipolar or whichever applicable illness. However, the more you can learn about it, the better because knowledge is power.

That being said, you will need to learn what the person's triggers are and how to help them avoid them or at the very least, help them cope with them when they do occur. I need you to remember something here for a moment too: You are *not* responsible for every little aspect of the afflicted person's life and you can only protect and help them as far as they would allow you to. They need to come to the party too. They need to become independent people as far as possible and learn to function in society as best as they possibly can. The best my wife can do for me when she sees a trigger situation coming on is to ensure that I take a Clobazam and many deep breaths; if it is more serious than just a temporary situation, she can also send me off to Dr M.

Finally, be patient with the person and give them the necessary space to cope with a diagnosis once it is made. Patience is an essential part of showing care. Give them the space to get over the initial shock of the diagnosis of mental illness. Patience means being there while they are trying to recompose themselves, and in some cases busy picking up the pieces of their world that fell apart when they were given a diagnosis. This isn't necessarily something that will happen overnight; bear in mind that it took me a long time to accept my diagnosis. That doesn't mean that you have to pick up their pieces for them but sometimes and more often than not in my experience, they may need a hand here and there. How the person puts themselves together is really none of your concern, but you need to speak up when you see them making a mistake.

It is likely that the person in question may suffer a relapse at some point and they may not be aware of it as it happens sometimes. Medication keeps Bipolar in check-up to a point, but then the symptoms may worsen to the extent that a healthcare professional needs to be called in again outside the scope of the routine check-ups of every three or six months. This is where the primary caregiver may come in: They need to be aware of the person's mood states and alert them to it, and if need be, also their psychiatrist. If you are going to look at the appendix of the book dealing with the different medicines, you may just see how important it is that you should monitor the person with Bipolar, especially if the patient is a teenager or a young adult. Relapse doesn't always mean hospitalisation. It mostly means an adjustment to a medication or therapeutic approach. I experienced that an adjustment in medication may often play havoc on a person, but it is a passing phase. Here your patience may again be called on, or even tested. More often than not, this adjustment phase lasts only a couple of days, but in the end, all turns out okay.

Chapter Eighteen

If you support someone with Bipolar

This chapter is intended for the primary caregivers of people who have Bipolar. I'm working on the assumption that a positive clinical diagnosis has been made. There are other psychiatric diseases which may present themselves similar to Bipolar, but they are in fact as different from each other as salt from sugar.

Like with the person who has Bipolar, you have one of two choices: To stand by your loved one or to distance yourself and leave them to their own devices. If you are reading this, I will assume that you have opted for the first choice, so please keep reading. If not, please take this book and chuck it in the closest dustbin because then it has meant nothing to you.

The first thing you need to know and understand is that we are not insane. We may become delusional and irrational at times, but that doesn't classify us as insane. Also, the lingering depressions are hard on you because it is basic human nature, especially as in a close relationship such as a romantic relationship, for the other party to wonder what they did wrong. You probably did nothing wrong, so don't take it personally. In fact, if you are reading this you are probably doing your level best to help and to understand. Kudos to you.

You, however, are the one who is outside looking in and believe me, there are days that we will need you to help us along. You will need to take us by the arm and lead us along as you would a blind person. There are times that your *eyesight* may be the only sight we'll have and therefore you have the difficult and sometimes unpleasant task of keeping our trust as I pointed out earlier.

People with Bipolar may think that there is very little reason to trust people, specifically for the reason that people tend to ostracise us because we are perceived as radically different and show unusual behaviours at times. Then there are also the stigmas that go hand-in-hand with Bipolar. Most people have heard of Bipolar before and just about everybody who has heard of it, has an opinion of those who have it, and it normally isn't good. Thank mass media for that.

We need to know that we can trust you and that you accept and love us, romantically or platonically, just the way we are. We need to know that you will stand by us, that you'll stay with us in the car no matter how rough the ride may get.

People with Bipolar are a handful and living in close proximity could mean anything from paradise the one day and the depths of hell the next. You need to be able to rely on your own inner strength and resources: We may not always be able to be there for you in the way you need us at a specific time. We may not always be able to laugh with you. Conversely, we may get irritated when you do not laugh with us. We may be bold and intrusive the one day but completely withdrawn the next, built into our own cold, impregnable stone fortresses.

Caregivers need care too. Speaking for myself, I tend to be suspicious and to be frank, I sometimes border on being a control freak and my wife sometimes has to explain her choices of caregivers to me. That brings me to another point: You must be able to stand your ground. Sometimes that may mean that you are not nice to the person with Bipolar. This may be because you are supporting something that is, as best you can see, in the person's best interest. You should be able to stand by it and maybe even defend yourself from our possibly irate and irrational responses.

There may also be the times when you may need to make their decisions for them. That may sometimes mean having some legal documents drawn up; a less than pleasant reality. In short, that will mean that the person with Bipolar may appoint you as a proxy over aspects in their lives they may be unfit to deal with, such as their finances.

The time may also come when the person with Bipolar needs to be hospitalised but refuses. By law, there are ways to get this done when it is an extreme case. This will be extremely hard on you and may, unfortunately, have long term repercussions on your relationship. In time your loved one ought to thank you when their reason returns, as it did with me after my second suicide attempt. I will say more about the different kinds of hospitalisation and intervention procedures later in the chapter.

It is vital that you should know the contact details of your loved one's professional caregivers – the psychiatrists and psychologists. I even recommend sitting in on a session or two with them. I have said earlier that it is important for a patient to feel comfortable with their professional caregivers, but I think it is equally important that you should know their professional caregivers at face value at least.

Also, be sure that you know what medication they take and in what dosages and the frequencies thereof. Know where they keep their medications: Check that they take it when they're supposed to, especially if they are experiencing an episode or if you suspect an episode is approaching, or worse – abusing their medication. Tranquilisers are absolutely divine, their effects are bliss, but some are also addictive. Check up on their stock levels once in a while: You may need to take the initiative to see that stocks are replenished. In the event of an intended overdose, it may also be useful if you could give an indication of the medications and the dosage to emergency response medical personnel. Keeping a day or two's supply of medication with you may always be a good idea; life has no guarantees and one never knows where one may end up without planning it.

I mentioned intentional overdose in the previous paragraph. It is an unfortunate and sad reality, a shocking fact actually, that one in about three people with Bipolar will attempt suicide. It is true that if the urge is strong enough, one will find a way to kill yourself. Try to limit the means of successful suicide as best you can. I still don't know how my ex managed it, but she got me to turn over my firearms to the police and I should thank her for that; not that I was elated at the time to do so.

There are, of course, other ways of reducing the suicide urge. The foremost is showing pure and unconditional love and acceptance and that the person with Bipolar is truly appreciated, regardless of their mental state.

In some cases, it may happen that you need to get a person admitted to a mental care hospital or clinic. This could happen voluntarily or involuntarily, depending on the person with Bipolar's psychiatric state. This doesn't only apply to Bipolar, but to all mental illnesses. In the case of voluntary admission of a person with medical aid to a private hospital or institution, there is no problem. However, there are times when a person, even with medical aid, needs to be admitted to a governmental institution Then things get tricky.

In South Africa, there are four categories of psychiatric admission:

The first is a voluntary admission: That is where a person seeks help out of their own free will and is admitted to a psychiatric hospital or institution for treatment as a person would voluntarily be admitted to any other hospital.

The second is an assisted admission: This happens when a person is, owing to their current mental state, unable to make an informed decision on treatment, yet does not refuse treatment. Such an assisted decision is typically made with the next of kin such as a spouse, or a parent or guardian if the person is younger than eighteen years on the date of application. The application must be made on the appropriate form (MCHA 4, available from governmental hospitals. For examples of such forms, you visit www.kznhealth.gov.za/townhill/forms.htm?)

Involuntary admission can happen when a person is unable to make an informed decision on treatment and refuses any needed treatment. The long and short of this is, as simple as I can try to explain it without all the legal jargon: This person is typically an endangerment to him/herself and others and needs rehabilitation to protect him/herself and others from physical or other sorts of harm, typically financially or by damaging his/her reputation.

Lastly, there are emergency admissions. It is also an involuntary admission. This is a tricky one since it may cause severe infringements of a person's human rights and is kept as a last alternative. Such an admission happens when any delay of admission may result in the death of the person by suicide, physical harm to others, permanent damage to own/other's property or when the person can cause serious harm to him/herself or others. In such a case, a person can be hospitalised for 48 hours for observation, when other serious medical and legal reviews will start, and the case will be duly handled according to the Mental Health Care Act (17 of 2003, as revised).

Like I pointed out, the matter of getting your afflicted loved one to professional care may obviously be a rough road. You may really have to bite down hard to do it sometimes and feel like you are severely hurting your loved one. You may feel that you aren't doing them a favour, but you actually are. They may not see it immediately; it may even take an extended period of time for them to realise that you did act in their best interest. There are no guarantees, though. Your loved one may never see it as a favour you did them and that may mean losing them.

But you lose them with a clear conscience if it comes to that.

PART FIVE

COMING BACK TO LIFE

Chapter Nineteen

A bumpy ride

Having Bipolar is nothing short of a bumpy ride in life. Sure, everybody's life is filled with ups and downs and surely people with Bipolar can't claim the bragging rights that it is only us that experience these ups and downs. *Normal* people experience ups and downs like waves on the ocean. So do people with Bipolar, but the difference is that sooner or later or dare I say more often than not, we experience tsunamis.

I think I have used enough analogies and metaphors in this book so far to describe the different ways of how people with Bipolar experience things as opposed to *normal* people. Unfortunately for you, I just find it easier to communicate in metaphors and analogies, so just bear with me for a little while longer, please.

This part of the book is titled *"Coming back to life."* When I initially started writing this book I was hospitalised for the first time and I thought it a good time to start working on fulfilling my life-long dream of publishing a book. I thought at the time that I had all the experience I needed to write a book on this matter.

Truth be told, I don't, and I doubt I ever will. As I said, I am no authority on Bipolar.

I expected that once I was discharged, both the first and the second time and even the third time around, everything will soon return to normal. I must admit, although I was wiser after my second admission, I am still eagerly waiting for that day where things are just magically normal, for want of a better expression. In the end, any day may be a setback and any day may be healing. You just never know which. Remember what I said about Eeyore and Tigger?

Therein lies the trickiness of Bipolar and like rough seas, it takes a seasoned captain to navigate them. What do I mean by navigation in this context? It means to be able to *anticipate*, *compensate* and *execute*.

There are many ways to learn what to anticipate from your Bipolar. One of the best ways widely recommended by psychiatrists and in literature is to keep mood journals, indicating your mood every day to try and establish a pattern of what you can expect next or in the foreseeable future. A friend suggested that you should also write down what happened to you during the day that made you feel a specific way. In so doing you will, with time, be able to accurately pinpoint your triggers.

I use mood journals, although I find that there is too much happening in my life and too many variables to make accurate estimations of what lies ahead. I have a fair idea from experience to know what my main triggers are: Stress of any kind, situations in which I exercise no degree of control over, overindulging in alcohol or the use of some medications like Codeine, cortisones and flu medicines containing ephedrine, pseudoephedrine and those kinds of ingredients, and a lack of sleep. Some of those lead to depression, some of them lead to mania. In my humble opinion, it is therefore more important to know what your triggers are and what reaction to anticipate.

Compensating yourself means applying your *ship's rudder* and turning your bow into the waves of the storm. That's right, it means facing it head-on. It doesn't matter how low you may feel; a ship is less likely to be capsized by waves when facing them. Similarly, when you're in a mania, you will feel that you are stronger than the storm, although you're not. You need to have coping strategies in place, and it doesn't matter how miserable or high you feel; it is okay if it is part of your coping strategy. And it is okay to flip over sometimes – most of us, like me, do sooner or later. There is help for times like those based on the proviso that you want to be helped, or you will go down like the Titanic.

What are the coping strategies I'm talking about? In the end all my coping strategies, whether I am in a manic phase or a depressive phase, all come down to functioning as normally as possible. To keep the game face on if you will. Yes, I feel very sorry for myself when depressed and I feel larger than life when manic, but it is all a matter of keeping things in perspective. It is a matter of keeping as busy as you can when depressed, it keeps your mind occupied with anything else than the swamp of tears and sorrow it is wading through. It is a matter of channelling your endless energy into something productive when manic. You'll be both shocked and amazed at how much you can achieve while you are manic. That is why it is said that people with Bipolar can be among the most creative, inventive and productive people on this planet.

What does it mean to execute? With Bipolar, I think it all comes down to action in the end. It means taking the appropriate actions at the right time and to know when to do a certain thing and to know when not to do the same thing. It means implementing your coping strategies at the right time. Do you remember that I mentioned that you can contemplate scenarios and how you will react to them? That is what I mean here: Executing those programmed responses.

Anticipate, compensate, execute.

Allow me to talk about some of my coping strategies. When I try to think of any, nothing springs to mind immediately apart from keeping busy. When I am depressed I try to keep my social interactions to the bare minimum. I talk only to the people have to when I need to. I answer the questions I am asked in short, concise answers. I put conscious effort into it not to bring everybody else down – a sour apple quickly turns other apples sour too. What it really comes down to is putting my soul in bed like one would put their body in bed when they're down with the flu. I allow my soul some time to rest as much as I can.

When manic things can turn very nasty very quickly, especially when my Borderline isn't playing along nicely. I get overly social when manic and say and do things I regret afterwards, especially when alcohol gets involved. Coping with mania and hypomania is harder than coping with depression for me. Other people with Bipolar may find it the other way around. To be completely frank with you, I don't really know how to cope with manias, simply because I don't get them that often anymore. During the time I had those raging manias I didn't even know I had Bipolar. Based on past experience, I know that I really have to work on it to keep my racing thoughts in check, simply because my mouth tends to work at the same ridiculous speed, if not faster. Also, I need to ensure I get sufficient sleep. I said earlier that you may feel rested after as little as two hours of sleep. Well, that's only a feeling, and feeling is often far removed from reality. I think that at any phase, sufficient rest is important if you have Bipolar; not too much and not too little.

Just by the way, did you notice TV in those lists? They're not there for a very good reason – TV suppresses activity in the frontal lobe of the brain, which is essential in combatting depression and mania. Getting that grey matter active should help you sort yourself out in a better time than wasting your life away in front of a TV set.

Chapter Twenty

Flirting with death

As with plenty of mental disorders, the risk of suicide in patients with Bipolar is extremely high. According to research conducted by SADAG, 50% of the whole population of people with Bipolar in South Africa have contemplated suicide, and a staggering 34% of people with Bipolar have attempted suicide.

Very few suicides, I call them movie suicides, are a matter of spiting or punishing someone in the sense that "I am killing myself, because you…", but where is the logic in that? Do I think that suicide is selfish? Ah, now we're moving on to the tricky questions, aren't we?

When we talk about voluntary euthanasia, you will have to exclude those pleading their mental condition to be to the extent that they pose a clear and present threat to the populace. Maybe you can use this dystopian future scenario and co-author a story with me – there are plenty of pieces of stories littering this mind, just dying to get out!

I have attempted suicide twice.

At the time of my first attempt, I was plagued by feelings of inadequacy as I didn't have a job at the time and I wasn't contributing to the household, much less fulfilling my role as the primary provider as I believe a husband should. I apologise for any feminists I may have offended now.

I was feeling tired at every level imaginable and I wanted to die for a long time by then, and I couldn't see any other way out of my situation. I was feeling like a burden to my family, both financially and emotionally, as I was progressively slipping into the darkest of depressions imaginable. People who live with those affected by Bipolar will be quick to confirm that it takes a lot of effort remaining standing and strong, and not let yourself get dragged down in your loved one's depressions. Many people with Bipolar will also tell you that they are aware of this fact.

I was beginning to see myself as a burden to myself, to my family and to society. I always said that if I was to become a burden to society in any way, people should let me die. I even wrote a living will, signed by witnesses, to that effect. That would, however, been applicable in an incident of severe physical injury, say, a motor vehicle accident.

I couldn't see how this would be any different – damage sustained in a suicide attempt or severe physical trauma. The long and short of it is that even if I survived the actual attempt, they would turn off the machines.

I didn't let anybody in on what was coming.

Although I didn't relish the thought of leaving anyone behind, I just couldn't bring myself to torment them the way I felt I was doing. I've been trying to stay strong for my family's sake for a long time, but by then I felt that I had nothing left to give. I had finally broken, and I didn't know how to fix myself. I felt that I had nothing left to contribute; that my usefulness had expired. It felt like a waste to me – all of it.

I wished that I had an impartial peer, even a complete stranger, to talk to. In a sense I wish that I had sought out the services of a counsellor, but who would understand? I was beyond the "pep talk", "say a little prayer", "good thoughts and vibes" thing. I was even feeling beyond God's help.

Things may have turned out differently if I talked to someone because I may have been able to get things off my chest and may have been at peace with myself and life as a whole. There were things I felt incapable of speaking to my wife. I knew that I wasn't providing, lacked direction in my life, was acutely aware of my life's pointlessness as I perceived it, and even felt that I wasn't doing enough at the time to get employed. Not even the retailers wanted me, let alone the kind of companies I was looking to get employed by. My relationships were falling apart. Those two things were always the defining pillars of my life: What I do, and my relationships. Both of these aspects were absent or failing during that time.

Then came the night I decided to test why my child's medications weren't helping and I took some of her Lorepazam (see appendix) which knocked me hard. The oblivion was bliss and I just decided to keep going and dove into my own Clobazam. It was a means of escape. I don't see the attempt as an accident because I was, as it is with most of my actions, very deliberate. It was a temporary relief that I tried to make permanent, even in my drugged state.

When writing about my first attempt, it was by no means as dramatic as I thought it would be. I just acted. Am I sorry about it? No, I'm not. Do I feel I could still look people in the eyes? Yes, I do. Looking back on it and standing a couple of steps back from it all, I think that those pills I took were a *bona fide* suicide attempt. How do I explain it all? Do I just say, "Hey, everybody. I tried to kill myself, but I survived?"

The second attempt was much more severe than the first. The only person I let on was a friend, to whom I only sent a couple of vague text messages.

At the time of my second suicide attempt, I was having an extramarital affair and I couldn't even look at myself in the mirror, much less to my wife looking at me being none the wiser. Although the affair was short-lived, it did, however, force me into leading a double life. I still don't know what I was thinking when I embarked on that affair – I could barely handle one life, so how could I even think about two?

Like the first attempt, the driving force behind my second attempt was also the need to escape. Only, with the second attempt, I had the huge burden of the guilt and shame because of my extramarital affair too. I really felt hopeless and what I had done was inexcusable in my frame of reference. Infidelity was way up on my list of unpardonable transgressions, only a short step behind rape and murder.

The long and short of it was this – I ended up taking around 300 tablets – mostly Loprazolam, several brands of benzodiazepines and Risperidone and ant poison – and woke up in ICU five days later. I spent another two weeks in hospital before being discharged.

Even though I survived two suicide attempts, I still don't feel quite qualified to talk about the mechanisms of it except that I was tired – physically, emotionally and mentally, and dealing with a lot of guilt and self-loathing. Many survivors, like me, say that the largest driving force behind any suicide is the urge to escape. When you get there, it is the only reality you know.

To me, both attempts were finally acting on what I've been feeling and thinking about for a long time. They were moments of madness where I was so tired of things not making sense anymore and the guilt I felt myself bearing.

I can't say that I was the most depressed I've ever been at the time of my first attempt. I've been through worse. I definitely wasn't depressed during my second attempt, but I was weighed down by the most unimaginable weight of guilt I thought existed.

I just reached those breaking points. It was points of hopelessness or feeling beyond atonement; there seemed to be no way out of it, except by dying.

I mention elsewhere that there is no means by which all the means to commit suicide can be completely removed, but only limited at best. I always knew that if I ever tried to commit suicide that it would be by means of an overdose of medications. I don't know why I never eliminated that means as I did with my firearms. I think I always thought of it as a fire escape and I suppose that I always thought of firearms as too messy and I didn't want anyone having to clean up after me.

My wife told me afterwards about things I did during both attempts that I wasn't aware of – apparently, you don't just lie down and die. Some other things happen in between. At my first attempt, I lost three days somewhere, including my birthday. She said I almost got physically violent towards her and toward our daughter during my second attempt. I have no I idea why I would have done that or what would have provoked me to do so – it is completely against my principles as a man. Was it the other guy driving again, as it was in my Varenicline phase?

Once a person has his or her mindset on committing suicide there is precious little you can do for them. The "pep talk" and "good vibes" or the "little prayer" doesn't work anymore by then. The best, if not the only thing you can do for such a person is to have them hospitalised on an Emergency Admission (see Chapter Eighteen). Then you had better pray that you get to such a person before they could actually commit suicide. When I attempted suicide the second time, I took the overdose, coolly said good-night and went to bed, nobody being any wiser. Sometimes there are really no physical warning signs.

It is therefore important to recognise the signs before the actual suicide is attempted. The problem with that is that each person's signals will vary. The common denominator is that the person acts outside of their normal characteristics – I had the affair. I became uncharacteristically withdrawn from my family – more so than I do at some other times. I had frequent outbursts of anger at work. So, the signs are very frequently difficult to pin-point as it was with mine, simply because they ranged over such a wide range of circumstances. Nobody had enough reason to expect that something was up, except for the friend I texted – but I don't blame him for not acting upon it; I have frequently sent him messages that I am very down, and I don't feel like living anymore. Make no mistake, I think very highly of him.

There are more common signs of suicide which bear mentioning because people often don't recognise these behaviours for what they are when they see them happening. When you see them, please act before it is too late. Ask the uncomfortable questions and be ready to be snubbed.

Here are some of the most common warning signs:

- ❖ A person may become overly depressed.
- ❖ A person may withdraw from relationships.
- ❖ A person may become obsessed with death and/or mention it, directly or indirectly.
- ❖ A person may start giving away items they attach value or sentiment to.
- ❖ A person may make a great effort to update their personal affairs such as wills and policies.
- ❖ A person may present with sleeping disturbances – either sleeping too much or too little.
- ❖ A person may suddenly resort to the use of alcohol or drugs.
- ❖ A person may suddenly present with reckless behaviour of any kind – sex, taking unprecedented risks such as gambling, reckless driving or suddenly and for apparent reason quitting a job.
- ❖ A person suddenly lies about many things.

As you can see, there are so many possible warning signs, more than I can possibly mention, that it is virtually impossible to keep track of all of them.

If you suffer from Bipolar, these things may serve as a barometer to you before you even realise that you are contemplating suicide. If you have a loved one battling mental disease I can only say take the skins off your eyes and keep a constant watch-out.

Chapter Twenty-One

Struggling with God

Since I don't know you, I have no idea what your religious views are. I don't even know whether you are even religious or not. It is by no means my intention to convert you to a particular religion in this chapter, neither is it a personal testimony, but I am striving to give an *exposé* of my own thoughts. This is a very dynamic topic to me; how I *feel* about the Creator changes almost every day.

Okay, so I used some taboo words in the book and I'm definitely no angel or saint, but God – I will refer to the Creator as God throughout this chapter as this is how I know Him, is important to me. I wouldn't struggle so much with God and the idea of God if it wasn't important to me.

If you don't believe in God and the afterlife, I do hope you'll keep reading. Even if you're an atheist, you can't deny that you've never thought about a Creator. I am not going to try to convince you of the existence of God, but please hear me out. I may just give you some things to think about and stuff that may serve as pointers somewhere down your road, or something that may at least serve as some form of philosophical amusement to you at the very least.

It is hard for me to pinpoint exactly what I am trying to achieve with this specific chapter. I am not trying to preach the Gospel to you, neither am I trying to sell you on religion – any religion for that matter.

To me, religion is dead – it is a set of rules and rituals to follow. Religiously you can do everything right but still not have a relationship with God.

I believe, for various reasons, that a relationship with God is important in dealing with Bipolar, even if it is a love-hate relationship. I think that God loves you unconditionally and any hate or hard feelings there may be is yours or mine.

I don't know, but I hypothesise that people with Bipolar have a harder time believing in God and trusting Him than most others. I can't know this as a fact because it is something I rarely discuss with other people with Bipolar, simply because it tends to be such a sensitive subject and can quickly spiral out of control. As for myself, my relationship with God is exactly what I imply in the title of this chapter: A struggle.

Many people believe for the mere reason that when they die, they want to go to Heaven. My first argument is this: As a person who suffers from Bipolar, why should I have reason to believe that I won't still have Bipolar should I get to Heaven, when it has just as much become a part of my soul as my body? My existence in this life can get pretty miserable for a considerable percentage of the time, so why should I believe it should be any different in the next? Eternity is a pretty long time to be miserable in. Should I believe that if I should get to Heaven I will be, for want of a better expression, magically healed? Actually, it doesn't matter to me.

It isn't even important to me whether I get to Heaven, or any form of afterlife for that matter or not. I don't believe in God as a one-way ticket to the blissful afterlife or some sort of Nirvana. It takes more than just faith to get there. The way I understand it is that faith must lead to deeds. I'm talking about actions like repentance from your wrongdoings.

I sometimes wonder if God is any more of a philosophical premise to me that I could use as a crutch to lean on when I need to because God isn't there to be used as you please. To me, God is very real, and I observe it in the entire universe around me: The wind on my skin, the laughter of a baby, the full moon hanging in the sky, to name but a precious few. My perceived universe doesn't make sense without a supreme being whom I call God and I believe in His true good and caring nature.

Why wouldn't the universe make sense to me without God? I find it hard to verbalise but I'll give it my best shot. I don't believe that the universe happened by accident. I see a Great Hand in it, as a master would complete a complex and beautiful painting. Secondly, when I look at the ingenuity of the workings of organic life, I stand amazed. Once again, I can't see how it just happened by accident. I will change that belief the day that the human race is able to create a living organism. God isn't a static concept to me. He is the perpetuator of life and the only One who can give it. Does he take it away? We can make our own choices leading to death. When someone commits suicide it isn't God who pulls the trigger.

You see, I see a divine order in the universe other than minds more brilliant than my own questioned. I don't see chaos in the natural order. I see a divine order and purpose, even though I don't always understand it. Maybe I believe like a child. Yet, that doesn't mean I don't question. Everybody knows that a child's most pressing question is *"Why?"*. You are more than welcome to accuse me of immature thinking, but believe me, I question all the time.

The most pressing questions we have in the human state when it comes to God is, *"If God is good, why is there evil?"* If he is all-knowing, why did he create Satan or by whichever name you call the evil one when he knew how much suffering it would lead to?" We may even take that question even further by asking, *"If God is good and means for us to have happy lives, why are there people who suffer from Bipolar?"* These are questions which are honestly beyond me. I can only theorise about them. I am no theologian and a very bad philosopher, but I can tell you what I believe.

I believe that God created all sentient beings with free will. The evil one chose to become as he is; in his arrogance and deceitfulness, instilled the same power lust in people when he successfully tempted mankind into a fall, thereby bringing every form of malady into this world. According to the Book I read, a single injustice justifies a life of pain and death. I'm talking about the injustices we commit against God, other people and especially the injustices we people with Bipolar are so prone to commit against ourselves. But I can't reasonably think of Bipolar as a punishment for our wrongdoings.

So, where does God come in with dealing with Bipolar in my case? I simply believe that I am in desperate need of the grace and mercy I am incapable of giving myself. Because he is good and loves me, he gives me grace and mercy, not that I by any means deserve it. He forgives me when I can't forgive myself. I sometimes need the comfort that no human being can offer me. I need peace in times of trouble and turmoil. I sometimes need strength I can't find within myself and I find that only in God.

That is a glimpse of my picture of God and the result of many years of believing, doubting, denying, hating and eventually accepting. My picture of God is in all probability very different from yours. To quote something from a wonderful writing called *Desiderata:* "Therefore be at peace with God, whatever you conceive him to be." I included that writing in Appendix Two of this book. I implore you to read it and if it resonates with you, make it your own.

Finally, there are enough stresses in fighting Bipolar. Don't let fighting with God be one of them.

Chapter Twenty-Two

Life with Bipolar, according to Nick

I am in no position to judge whether life is harder or easier for people who don't have to live with Bipolar every day of their lives, although the obvious answer would be to believe that it is a simpler life for them. However, I can't judge because I have never experienced it. My wife often asks the question, "What is normal anyway?" Do we folks with Bipolar actually have it figured out or are we, along with so many of us with mental afflictions, maybe society's cracked nuts?

I think it all comes down to a matter of perception, but most of the times we judge our days as either good or bad. There are the days we feel on the up but in a bad way. Some others we feel down, but it isn't bad. So, how can feeling down not be bad? There are just so many questions without answers in Bipolar!

At the core, I think we are still human. Contrary to how we may feel on some days, we are not waiting for a mother ship. We have the same emotions as the next person. We interact, we react. A certain emotional trigger is likely to illicit relatively the same emotional response albeit in an amplified or attenuated degree.

As a person, I generally prefer to be withdrawn from other people for obvious reasons. I learnt to prefer being an observer, not a participant any further than I need to be. I like watching people, studying them and come to conclusions about how I perceive them to be. That may or may not be a matter of cutting myself off from other people or the world that hurt me so much, but it is equally amusing to me as well and a self-defense mechanism.

So, how do I perceive the world to be and what about life itself? I once said to a friend that life is cruel and intolerably strange. The world is a hard place and there is no room for sissies in it. No matter who you are, if you want to survive, whatever your perception of survival is, you had better step up to the base and play ball, all the while remembering that life has but one guarantee and that is that you are going to die.

Yes, there is a great level of stigma clinging to Bipolar as it is with all other mental conditions ranging from depression to schizophrenia. People often simply can't or won't accept that a person is mentally ill. Some people, in fact, think we are merely just insane or full of shit. People fear what they don't understand and people especially fear to have to explore the arcane realm of mental disorders.

The most difficult part to me is that many people don't understand that I am ill when I appear fine physically. I don't have a runny nose or watery eyes; I don't complain of a sore tummy and I'm not vomiting. Instead, I may just hang my head or cover my ears. I may be fine in all aspects on one day and then be off from work on sick leave for three days, just to appear back at work looking as fine as the day before I left. People generally do not understand this and cannot accept it. If they but knew the inner workings, they would be able to understand that in those three days a literal struggle for life and death took place. That happens with me from time to time when I begin to feel suicidal.

That brings me to the question of how and when you die and how you'll be remembered. There are those who believe that our days are numbered, and the day and time of our death is a predestined thing. I agree with that because I am a believer. However, in that lies a conundrum: Your life is in the hands of your Creator. But any time you choose, you can end your it. Or try to, at least. Neither of my attempts, it would seem, was my time.

If you have Bipolar, or one of the many other mental disorders for that matter, you will most likely be familiar with that deep dark hole where there seems to be no difference between life and death anymore. I have been there enough times and if it wasn't so dark there, I could have drawn you a map of it. That is the place where you cut and burn yourself to see if you are still alive and relish physical pain – if you bleed and feel pain, you must still be alive. It is when you cannot feel physical pain anymore that the line between life and death becomes blurry and the barrel of a gun starts looking very friendly to you. It starts to look like a sweet release from the hell you are living in: Death cannot be worse than it. At that point nothing matters anymore: You don't have the will or energy or clarity to think of things like what your suicide will do to those you leave behind and other considerations of the kind. Escaping by death is your only way out and your only reality.

That is why you need to think about these things while you are of a clear mind. As for me, I would like to go out with a bang someday. Hard and fast without suffering while doing something I enjoy. That is why you need to find the things you enjoy and actually do them. They make you feel good when you are down, and they take the edge off when you are feeling too hyper.

How you will be remembered isn't entirely up to you. You can, however, influence that by your daily life and the decisions you make. You will be remembered by the quality of the life you lived: Will you always give your best, no matter how hard it gets? Will you, on some days, pick yourself up by your shoelaces when all appears hopeless, as best you can? Will you always treat people to the best that your mood state allows you to? Will you, in the face of all adversity, still give your best? That is *character,* and people are remembered by that.

See, since each case of Bipolar is so unique, not everybody is going to get the same things in their *lucky packet.* I like calling it a lucky packet for the reason that there are sweets and nice things in it to eat, but also a lot of cheap *Made in China* junk: Any manner of trinket imaginable, the one more useless than the next. Or at least then, stuff you will have a hard time finding a sensible use for.

The same is true with Bipolar: We all get our lucky packet and sometimes it even gets mixed up that a boy gets a girl's packet or the other way around in the party which is life. There are two rules with that lucky packet which is different from any other lucky packet: You can't throw it away, neither can you swap with someone else. That lucky packet you've been handed is yours to stay and you will take it to your grave with you. All of it, even the *Made in China* stuff.

So you might as well find out what is in it. Of course, there will be the nice parts or the sweets, and there will be the less pleasant parts like the small, prickly hair clips reeking of moulded plastic and who knows what else; stuff that normally gets lost within hours or days, never to be thought of again.

By the way – I am so sorry if I am spoiling lucky packets for you here.

The cruel part of it is that normally we can have only the sweets or the other junk at any one time. You cannot, like a child, cry and throw a tantrum at someone because they came and took away the sweets and gave you the nasty trinkets to play with again.

Everybody knows that eating too many sweets can cause sugar rushes but not getting enough sugar also has adverse effects. Playing is good, even with cheap toys. Playing with them until they hurt you or others with them isn't.

You have to open that lucky packet to see what's inside to know what you're dealing with. I believe that with it comes some kind of route map, directions or at the very least pointers and signs if you will.

On the lucky packet is a "Caution!" sign warning you that there is trouble. Open it and the second sign is a T-junction sign: That is the sign where you have to choose the denial or the existence of your condition. If you turn to the route of denial like I did at first, the road signs you see will few and far between and inaccurate. Luckily U-turns are allowed.

If you choose the road to acceptance, one of the first signs you'll see is a sign telling you how far it is to the nearest service station; the other possible one is a "you are here" map. Both these signs have it in common, and that is that they will point you in a direction to where you can get help.

This road has information signs, warning signs, advisory signs, and even speed limits. The problem with Bipolar is that the road doesn't always allow for a constant cruising speed simply because the road surface isn't always the same. You cannot go at 120 kilometres per hour on loose sand, but neither is there any reason to go at 40 kilometres per hour on a tarred, four-lane highway.

By all means, open your lucky packet. Do not be afraid. It is your own personal treasure chest. You need to let it all out, not slamming the lid on it and leaving only hope trapped inside that lucky packet of yours.

Because there is always hope. What hope, you may ask.

My friend, as you are reading this, you have survived 100% of what life has thrown at you. That is a pretty good track record. Keep going at it. You will *always* pull through as long as you have the will and hope, no matter how small. You weren't born to be a loser. I don't think anybody is. Losers don't look for help, and reading this book also means that you want to help yourself too, or at the very least looking for things you can relate to.

As for me, I would like to be remembered in the first place as a good husband, better than I've been, to my wife, a good father to my children and as someone who offered people hope and shone a light for people in dark places, hence this book.

Ultimately life is a journey, and life with Bipolar is probably a slightly more intricate one. Unfortunately, the guy who drives like an ass is still out there, even on the fair paths, waiting to hijack me. Robert Frost in a poem wrote about a road that split in two in a forest; one clear and fair and the other overgrown and rough. My journey is on the latter. It forces me to live a life less ordinary.

My name is Nick and I am a survivor, no matter what I have done.

Because it is a choice I make every day.

Further reading

As I said in the book, knowledge is key to understand and battle Bipolar. Here are some worthwhile resources which may also prove helpful to you:

The National Institute for Mental Health (http://www.nimh.gov) is the American government's website for mental illnesses. It contains invaluable information on recognising and dealing with Bipolar and is where I also found a lot of statistics and technical stuff I used in this book.

If you are on Facebook, there is a wealth of pages on Bipolar and support groups. Just do a quick search and you will find them. I think, however, that it will be unethical of me to point you directly towards them as this may be counted as advertising and I'm certain not all the page and group administrators will thank me for that.

BP Magazine for Bipolar (http://www.bphope.com) contains many articles, blogs, and columns on other people's experiences with the illness and I often learn something I didn't know just about every day.

The South African Depression and Anxiety Group (SADAG) is a locally-based non-profit organisation, where you may also find a wealth of articles on Bipolar and other mental illnesses. They can also point you in the direction of support groups if you feel the need for them. SADAG's website is http://www.sadag.org.

Several books exist on the matter of Bipolar and I can't really point out any of them specifically to you but three:

"An Unquiet Mind" and "Touched with Fire" by Kay Redfield Jameson, MD: The first is the memoir of her life leading up to and after her diagnosis with Bipolar and is much more elaborate and informative than my own descriptions in this book. The latter is about the creative impulse of people with Bipolar and an inspiring read. It was also recently adapted into a motion picture by the same title.

"A Brilliant Madness: Living with Manic-Depressive Illness" by Patty Duke and Gloria Hochman is about the once-famous childhood star and actress and her battle against Bipolar. Each of Patty's experiences is backed up with technical medical facts. It was a bit of a cumbersome read to me but worth it in the end.

Appendix 1

Medications

Be warned that this is a rather technical part, which is why I rather opted to put it as an appendix so if you don't feel like reading this, it's okay. It may still be useful reading as I try to convey as much relevant information in lay terms as I can about the different treatments used, especially about the unpleasant side effects that may be experienced. The only reason I include this part in this book is that there may be persons, like myself, who like to know what I put into my body and what side effects to expect from them.

Bipolar patients are very seldom treated with an anti-depressant only, as this could push the patient into mania as the anti-depressant only relieves the symptoms of depression, psychologically and physiologically. Treatment with an anti-depressant is likely to occur only during acute treatment for depression phases in Type II Bipolar and in conjunction with another mood stabiliser *and* under the close supervision of the psychiatrist.

The long and short of medication in Bipolar is that the optimal medications and dosages must be determined. It is said that each Bipolar patient's *cocktail* of medications and dosages are as unique as they are. The only thing people need to keep in mind with medication is that it takes time to find the correct regimen of treatment. Things will more than likely get worse before they get better, and there may be a boo-boo or two in the process.

In Bipolar, three main clinical treatment phases apply: Acute, continuation, and maintenance.

Acute treatment is used typically during episodes and relapses and aims to suppress the symptoms of the episode, typically a severe depression, mania, hypomania or mixed cycle. It is in acute treatment where you will experience the most side-effects and you may feel that the medications aren't working, simply because your body must still adapt to them. Continuation treatment aims to prevent the return of a symptom or symptoms from a prior episode of acute treatment. Maintenance treatment aims to prevent the repetition of symptoms and is used when a patient is in remission.

Most drugs used in the treatment of Bipolar should be avoided during pregnancy and breastfeeding. If you are pregnant or planning to become pregnant, it is best to discuss the medicines with your psychiatrist. Also note that most of the medicines used in the treatment of Bipolar are also indicated in the treatment of other conditions, foremost epilepsy and schizophrenia. The fact that you may be treated with such medications doesn't make you an epileptic or schizophrenic any more than being covered in icing sugar make you a cake.

The side effects of medications are the reason most people want to quit theirs – that is, what it feels to you the medication is doing. Try to look past the side effects. Discuss them with your psychiatrist or have your psychiatrist discuss them with you.

Medicines used in the treatment are divided into several categories. I am including several antidepressants into this list as they may be used to treat cases where severe depression is present.

Mood stabilisers, the most important pharmaceutical treatment aspect of Bipolar, are typically anti-epileptics, atypical antipsychotics and some benzodiazipines to relieve the symptoms of anxiety, or just to take the edge off sometimes.

Although I list plenty of side effects to treatments it is not to say that you will experience any or all of them. They are just the most common ones reported in clinical trials and the percentages of these side effect reported are actually quite low; the side effects listed only occurred in 20% or more of participants during clinical trials of the specific medicine. If you experience any of these side-effects it is best to report it to your psychiatrist. In some of the cases, I add the black-box warning used in the US as it contains very clear indications of the dangerous side-effects some of these medications may have.

The medicines listed are according to the South African pharmaceutical formulary and may be different in your country. I should also point out that the information contained in this appendix is strictly according to my own research and the technicalities may not at all times be entirely accurate.

*   *   *

Aripiprazole is an atypical antipsychotic used in the treatment of manic and mixed manic episodes. Its most common side effects are headaches and weight gain.

In the US Aripiprazole carries a black box warning. This means that the drug has potentially harmful side effects and contraindications. Aripiprazole can lead to an increased risk of death due to cardiovascular failure and infectious diseases such as pneumonia.

Carbamazepine is a mood stabiliser and anti-epileptic used to suppress the effects of mania and hypomania. It is also one of many medications indicated for Bipolar that is also an anti-epileptic. It is known to cause dizziness, drowsiness, and nausea.

In the US, Carbamazepine carries a black box warning about serious dermatological reactions like rashes and acne.

Citalopram is used to treat severe depression and in the SSRI (Selective Serotonin Update Inhibitor) category. You will probably find yourself on it during acute treatment for a major depressive episode. Reported side effects include dry mouth and nausea.

In the US, Citalopram carries a black-box warning as it is known to increase the risk of suicidal thinking in children, adolescents, and young adults. Any behavioural changes and suicidal tendencies should be reported to the psychiatrist.

Clobazam is an anti-anxiety agent and a tranquiliser, falling in the benzodiazepine category. Being used as tranquiliser mainly, it will obviously cause drowsiness. It has also been reported that it may cause a rise in body temperature.

Clozapine is an atypical antipsychotic used to reduce recurrent suicidal behaviour in patients who show resistance to other atypical antipsychotics. The frequencies of side effects have not been determined but it may cause lowered blood pressure, fever, increased appetite and gastric discomforts.

In the US, Clozapine carries a black-box warning. It may increase the risk of infections, seizures, adverse cardiovascular side effects, and severe dizziness.

Escitalopram is an anti-depressant and belongs in the SSRI category and closely related to Fluoxetine. It is also used for anxiety disorders, OCD and insomnia. It has fewer side effects than Fluoxetine but most commonly they include headaches and nausea and ejaculation disorders in some cases.

In the US, Escitalopram carries a black-box warning. It has shown an increased risk of suicidal thinking in teenagers, young adults, and geriatrics. It should not be used to treat Bipolar by itself – a mood stabiliser should be prescribed with it. Patients must be closely monitored for changes in behaviour and this should be communicated to the patient's psychiatrist as soon as possible.

Flupentixol is a typical antipsychotic usually used to treat depression, with or without anxiety. In higher dosages, it is also used to treat schizophrenia. Its action is similar to that of tranquilisers such as Clobazam.

Its most common side effects include abnormal movements, changes in menstrual cycles, decreased sexual interest or function, swelling of breasts and muscle spasms.

Fluoxetine is indicated in the treatment of major depressive episodes, OCD and panic disorders to list a few, and belongs to the SSRI category of medications. It has, unfortunately, many unpleasant side effects, such as headaches, nausea, insomnia, diarrhoea, and weakness. The list is quite long.

In the US, Fluoxetine carries a black-box warning. It has shown an increased risk of suicidal thinking in teenagers, young adults, and geriatrics. It should not be used to treat Bipolar by itself – a mood stabiliser should be prescribed with it. Patients must be closely monitored for changes in behaviour and this should be communicated to the patient's psychiatrist as soon as possible.

Fluvoxamine belongs to the SSRI category of medicines. It is mainly used in the treatment of OCD. It is known to cause headaches, nausea, sleepiness but also insomnia and weakness.

In the US, Fluvoxamine carries a black box warning as it is known to increase the risk of suicidal thinking in children, adolescents, and young adults. Any behavioural changes and suicidal tendencies should be reported to the psychiatrist.

Gabapentin is an anti-epileptic mainly used along with other medicines in treatment. It can be said that it is used to suppress the side effects of other medications. Its own side effects may include dizziness and sleepiness.

Lamotrigine is an anti-epileptic typically used in the treatment and prevention of depression and is also a mood stabiliser. Side effects may include visual disturbances, clumsiness and skin rash, mental afflictions such as anxiety, confusion, and irritability. It is very often used in conjunction with Valproic acid as they work in synergy to create a very effective combination of mood stabilisers.

In the US, Lamotrigine carries a black-box warning. It may cause severe dermatological effects, even to the point of requiring hospitalisation.

Lithium is a very popular drug used in the treatment of Bipolar. It is said to have the best effect in suppressing and preventing manic episodes and decreasing the risk of suicide and self-harm. Lithium commonly causes dry mouth and thirst, muscle tremor and weakness, headache and dizziness, poor memory and confusion and gastrointestinal discomforts. Less common side effects are acne and hair loss. When treated with lithium, the patient needs to have blood tests administered frequently, because optimal levels need to be maintained and metal poisoning avoided which makes Lithium a tricky drug to use.

Lurasidone is an atypical antipsychotic used to treat major depressive cycles in Bipolar. It may cause drowsiness, restlessness, and nausea.

In the US, Lurasidone carries a black box warning as it can cause an increased risk of suicidal thinking in children, adolescents, and young adults also taking antidepressants. Any behavioural changes and suicidal tendencies should be reported to the psychiatrist.

Lorazepam is a benzodiazepine used to relieve anxiety disorders and short-term insomnia. It is basically a strong tranquiliser. It has quite a long list of side effects but as a tranquiliser it will obviously cause drowsiness, unsteadiness, sedation, fatigue, and amnesia.

Mirtazapine is used in the treatment of depression. Its side effects include sleepiness and dry mouth.

In the US, Mirtazapine carries a black-box warning as it is known to increase the risk of suicidal thinking in children, adolescents, and young adults. Any behavioural changes and suicidal tendencies should be reported to the psychiatrist.

Olanzapine is an antipsychotic used to treat major manic episodes in Bipolar. It is often used in conjunction with Valproic acid or Lithium. It may also be used along with Fluoxetine in cases of depression. You may experience weight gain, drowsiness, head rushes, weakness, increased cholesterol levels, and some movement disorders.

In the US, Olanzapine carries a black box warning as it can contribute to cardiovascular or infectious diseases. It may cause severe sedation and even coma in the case of injections. However, Olanzapine is normally tablets taken orally.

Oxcarbazepine is an anti-epileptic mainly used along with other medicines in the treatment. It can be said that it is used to suppress the side effects of other medications. It has quite a long list of side effects including dizziness, visual disturbances, headaches, nausea, sleepiness, and motor function impairments.

Paliperidone is an atypical antipsychotic used in conjunction with antidepressants or mood stabilisers. Its side effects may include sleepiness but also insomnia, restlessness, headaches and rapid heart rate.

In the US, Paliperidone carries a black-box warning as it increases the risk of infectious and cardiovascular diseases.

Paroxetine is among other a broad-spectrum antidepressant belonging to the SSRI class of medicines. It is used to treat a big variety of conditions, such as depression, OCD, panic disorders and PTSD, to name but a few. Side effects may include nausea, insomnia, dry mouth, headaches, constipation or diarrhoea, dizziness and ejaculation disorders.

In the US, Paroxetine carries a black-box warning as it may increase the risk of suicidal thinking and changes in behaviour in children, adolescents, and young adults. This should be closely monitored, and the psychiatrist informed if this should occur.

Quetiapine is an atypical antipsychotic used in the treatment of depression in Bipolar but is also used as a maintenance medication. Its side effects include dry mouth, increased blood pressure, drowsiness, dizziness, and headaches.

In the US, Quetiapine carries a black-box warning as it is known to increase the risk of suicidal thinking in children, adolescents, and young adults. Any behavioural changes and suicidal tendencies should be reported to the psychiatrist.

Risperidone is an atypical antipsychotic used in the treatment of mania in Bipolar, normally over a short period of time. It has many undesired side effects, most commonly drowsiness but also insomnia, increased appetite, agitation, fatigue, urinary incontinence, vomiting, and Parkinsonism most commonly.

In the US, Risperidone carries a black-box warning as it may increase the risk of cardiovascular and infectious diseases.

Sertraline is an antidepressant in the SSRI class of medicines. It is used in the treatment of major depressive episodes, OCD, panic and anxiety disorders, and PTSD. Side effects include headaches, insomnia, diarrhoea, and nausea.

In the US, Sertraline carries a black-box warning as it is known to increase the risk of suicidal thinking in children, adolescents, and young adults. Any behavioural changes and suicidal tendencies should be reported to the psychiatrist.

Topiramate is an anti-epileptic used to limit the onset of partial seizures. It can be said that it is used to suppress the side-effects of other medications. Its own side effects may most commonly include dizziness and blood serum ailments.

Trazodone is an anti-depressant and is subsequently used as such. Side effects include headaches, dizziness, drowsiness, dry mouth, and nausea.

In the US Trazodone carries a black-box warning as it is known to increase the risk of suicidal thinking in children, adolescents, and young adults. Any behavioural changes and suicidal tendencies should be reported to the psychiatrist.

Valproic acid is an anti-epileptic used to suppress mania. The most common side effects include nausea, increased bleeding time, tremors, headaches, drowsiness, increased risk of infections, hair loss, weakness, and sleepiness.

In the US, Sodium valproate carries a black-box warning as it can cause life-threatening liver failure and pancreatitis.

Vortioxetine is an anti-depressant and is used as such. Its most common side effect is nausea.

In the US Vortioxetine carries a black-box warning as it is known to increase the risk of suicidal thinking in children, adolescents, and young adults. Any behavioural changes and suicidal tendencies should be reported to the psychiatrist.

Ziprasidone is an atypical antipsychotic used for the treatment of manic and mixed manic phases, typically in patients with Type I Bipolar. Its most common side effect is motor function disorders.

In the US, Ziprasidone carries a black-box warning as it has shown an increased risk for cardiovascular and infectious diseases.

Appendix 2

Desiderata

Whether you are familiar with this piece of writing or not, it is worth looking over it from time to time because of the good advice it contains. I have found that, on the road of Bipolar, it is of great help to me. It is like sitting down by a fire and listening to the wisdom of a very wise man. Even others who do not have Bipolar can also learn plenty from it. This piece is not copyright protected, so feel free to use it anywhere and anytime you like.

*　　　*　　　*

Go placidly among the noise and haste and remember what peace may be in silence.

As far as possible, without surrender, be on good terms with all people. Speak your truth quietly and clearly; and listen to people, even to the dull and ignorant, they too have their story. Avoid loud and aggressive persons, they are vexations to the spirit.

If you compare yourself to others, you may become vain and bitter; for always there will be greater and lesser persons than yourself. Enjoy your achievements and keep your plans.

Keep interested in your own career, however humble; it is a real fortune in the changing fortunes of time.

Exercise caution in your business affairs, for the world is full of trickery. But let this not blind you to what virtue there is; many people strive for high ideals and everywhere life is full of heroism. Be yourself. Especially do not feign affection. Neither be cynical about love, for in the face of all aridity, it is perennial as the grass.

Take kindly the counsel of the years, gracefully surrendering the things of youth. Nurture strength of spirit to shield you in sudden misfortune. But do not distress yourself with dark imaginings. Many fears are born of fatigue and loneliness.

Beyond a wholesome disciple, be gentle with yourself. You are a child of the universe, no less than the trees and stars; you have a right to be here. And whether it is clear to you or not, no doubt the universe is unfolding the way it should.

Therefore be at peace with God, whatever you conceive Him to be, and whatever your labours and aspirations, in the noisy confusion of life, keep peace in your soul.

With all its sham, drudgery and broken dreams, it is still a beautiful world.

Be cheerful. Strive to be happy.

This is one of the first pieces I've ever read since I started reading in English and of all, made the biggest impact in my life. I trust you will also take something worthwhile from it.